Dessert Mash-Ups

by Dorothy Kern
blogger at *Crazy for Crust*

Ulysses Press

For Jordan, my #1 taste tester and little superstar.
And for Mel, without whom this adventure would not be possible.

Published in the U.S. by
Ulysses Press
P.O. Box 3440
Berkeley, CA 94703
www.ulyssespress.com

ISBN: 978-1-61243-365-3
Library of Congress Control Number 2014932299

Printed in the United States by Bang Printing

10 9 8 7 6 5 4 3 2 1

Acquisitions Editor: Katherine Furman
Editor: Lauren Harrison
Proofreader: Mary Hern
Design and layout: Ashley Prine
Indexer: Jay Kreider, J S Editorial
Photographs: © Dorothy Kern except on page 152 © Kirkpatrick Photography

Distributed by Publishers Group West

Contents

Get in on the fun by posting pictures to Instagram using #dessertmashups and tagging @crazyforcrust!

Introduction

I love crust. Those three words are what inspired me to start my blog, Crazy for Crust, back in 2010. The crust is my favorite part of the pie, and it deserved to be showcased and loved. I didn't think that crust was getting enough attention; it was usually reserved for pie, and pie was reserved for Thanksgiving. I felt something needed to be done about that. So I started crazyforcrust.com, figuring the pie lovers would find me and together we would make crust as mainstream as the cupcake.

Shortly after embarking on my blogging journey, I realized that I wanted to bake more than just pie. I loved all desserts! So one day I made what I called a Shortbread "Piookie," a shortbread cookie that looked like a pie. I filled it with chocolate ganache, took some horrible photos, and posted my very first dessert mash-up. I had no idea that one day I'd be writing a whole cookbook about putting two desserts into one delectable recipe.

Over the next few years, I discovered how much fun it was to put two desserts together into one amazing treat. Regular chocolate chip cookies were old news; every blogger had already done that. I needed to find something new, some recipe that hadn't already been written and passed around a thousand times. And more often than not, those recipes were mash-ups. Brownies with crust, blondies in pie, cake flavors in ice cream, pie flavors in Rice Krispies treats, s'mores anything. Standing in the candy aisle at the grocery store became a new adventure. What could I make with Reese's Peanut Butter Cups? What could I make that tastes like a Snickers? And, most importantly, what could I add crust to next? It was like a challenge—a big, fun, sugary baking experiment.

And then the mash-up became more than just a Pinterest and blog phenomenon; it became a household word. One little breakfast item, the Cronut, put the dessert mash-up on the map. With its launch in May of 2013, the Cronut became one of the most talked-about desserts in history. What was at one time thought to be strange and somewhat outrageous, eating two desserts in one, is now not only acceptable, it's almost expected. My adding crust to fudge and stuffing truffles in brownies didn't seem like it was so "out there" anymore. (Thank goodness!)

The idea of writing a cookbook about dessert mash-ups wasn't so surprising to me: It's what I do every day. I think it's one of the most creative ways to make dessert; you're not just making a cookie, you're making it taste like an apple pie. What can you add to that pie to make it taste like a chocolate chip cookie? Or add to that coffee cake to make it taste like carrot cake? It's letting your brain run wild with ideas and then turning them into a sweet reality.

Throughout the pages of this book you'll find some of my favorite mash-ups. Enjoy a Scout for breakfast, or maybe a slice of Milky Way Brownie Pie for dessert. I hope that you adore all of them as much as I do. Find some cookies that you love, some candy you have to have, and a cheesecake that's calling your name. Then do a double take, because you might be seeing two desserts where you thought there was just one.

Baking Equipment

I'm not a trained chef, but I've been baking since I could stand on a chair and stir brownie batter with a spoon. My mom had lots of bowls and wooden spoons in her kitchen, but no fancy equipment. We lived by her hand mixer, the blender was only seen when we were making banana bread, and I think I can count on one hand the times I saw her pull out the food processor.

When I was registering for my wedding several years ago, a whole new world of baking tools opened up to me. I remember walking through Bed, Bath, and Beyond with my scanning gun, my eyes big and mouth agape looking at it all, wanting all the things, and that was just the gadget wall. Then, in the early 2000s, the Food Network made me realize there were even more tools I needed. A whisk isn't just something chefs use. I needed one too. Better yet, I needed three.

Over the past several years of writing my blog, it's felt like I've baked enough for two lifetimes. In that time I've had lots of practice with kitchen appliances and gadgets alike, and I've come to find my favorites, the ones that I cannot live without, and the ones that just aren't necessary (I'm looking at you, cupcake corer).

In writing this book, I used my favorite baking equipment, so I thought I'd share my must-haves. If you're reading through any of the recipes and question something I'm using, just check back here. If you don't have it, you can probably find it at Target, on Amazon, at Sur la Table, or at Kohl's (my four favorite places to shop). Leave a little sticky note for your significant other, and maybe you'll come home to a bouquet of offset spatulas one day. You never know . . .

Pans

It's really important to have a wide range of baking pans. And, just a little tip, get two of each. There is nothing worse than needing to make a cake and realizing you only have one 9-inch round pan. Then you have to bake half a cake, let it cool, and bake the second half. Think of pans like shoes: They should come in pairs.

My must-have baking pans:
- 8 x 8-inch square
- 9 x 9-inch square
- 9 x 13-inch rectangular
- 9-inch round
- Springform pan (9- to 10-inch)
- Cookie sheets
- Jelly roll pan (10 x 15-inch rectangular)
- 9-inch pie plate
- Standard-size cupcake or muffin pan (12-cup)
- Mini cupcake or muffin pan (12- to 24-cup; it's good if you have a total of 48 cups because mini recipes usually make a lot)

Gadgets & Appliances

For a while, I was a gadget freak. Slicers, dicers, juicers, special spoons, special forks, special cutters and corers—you name it, I bought it. But then, most of these specialty items would end up in the back of the jumbled gadget drawer. Instead of using them, I'd just curse them because they'd make the drawer stick when I tried to open it.

But then some gadgets, even though you don't use them often, are awesome. Take a strawberry huller, for instance. I don't use it very much, but if you're hulling a large amount of berries (like for the Strawberry Pie Cupcakes, page 87, or the Chocolate-Covered Strawberry Truffles, page 122), it just makes life easier. Some gadgets, like the aforementioned cupcake corer, just end up taking up space I could fill with measuring spoons. Pick and choose your favorites, the ones you end up going back to over and over. Get rid of the rest; your drawers will thank you.

My must-have gadgets and appliances:

Wooden Spoons and Silicone Spatulas.
Just like in my mom's kitchen, I love a good wooden spoon for stirring. Wooden spoons aren't good for pouring from a bowl into a pan, so I have lots and lots (and lots) of spatulas too.

Measuring Cups and Spoons.
This is a given, and you probably have them already. But do yourself a favor: Get at least two sets of each. There's nothing worse than scooping out a cup of peanut butter and then realizing you need 2 cups of flour.

Cookie Scoops.
If you're still scooping cookie dough the old-fashioned way, between two spoons, you need a cookie scoop. Actually, you need at least three. These mini ice cream scoops are perfect for scooping equally sized balls of cookie dough. They come in several sizes, but you need at least my three favorites: 1 tablespoon (perfect for a mini cookie), 2 tablespoon (for a good-sized cookie), and $1/4$ cup (for filling cupcake and muffin liners). If you buy one gadget as a result of this book, let it be a cookie scoop.

Candy Thermometer.
It's scary seeing these two words in a recipe. Am I right? But you know what? Using the candy thermometer isn't scary at all! The scary thing is trying to make a recipe without one by timing it instead and hoping it's done right. The thermometer takes out the guesswork. It's great for candy and also for frying. It's a double-duty item!

Silicone Baking Mats.
I first discovered the Silpat silicone baking mat when watching Food Network. (I may not have gone to pastry school, but I definitely could get a degree in food-TV watching!) The chefs used them for baking cookies and it took me a long time to fork over the $25 for one. But it's the best money I ever spent! I now have three, and ask for more each Christmas. They're reusable, nonstick, and great for cookies or anything sticky. I bake every single cookie on them, unless they've already been used and need a washing. Then I use parchment paper, which I also love, but that gets expensive fast. The silicone pays for itself after one holiday baking season, I assure you.

Offset Spatulas. Remember back in the day when you'd ice a cake with really long flat icing spatulas? Yeah, I do too. I hated it. They never worked right for me, ever. One day early on in my Food Network–watching days, someone (probably Sandra Lee) pulled out an offset spatula to frost a cupcake. It's a shorter version of an icing spatula, and it's offset, meaning that the spatula part is lower than the handle. That offset part makes all the difference when doing so many things in the kitchen. I have two of these wondrous gadgets and I use them for everything from frosting cupcakes and cakes (like the Death by Chocolate Brownie Cake, page 83) to spreading chocolate on candy bark (like the Brownie Peppermint Bark, page 146). Pretty much a week doesn't go by that I don't use them at least once.

Aluminum Foil. Now, it's a toss-up if this is a gadget or a pantry staple, but I use foil like it's a cooking appliance. If I'm making brownies or bars, or anything that I want to remove from the pan to cut, I line the pan with foil. It makes for easy removal and pretty cuts (especially important for taking pictures for a food blog!) And, as a bonus, it leaves your pan clean. If you can keep a secret . . . sometimes I don't even wash the pan after. Foil = fewer dishes. That's a happy day for me.

Hand Mixer. This is my old standby. You can do pretty much anything with a good electric hand mixer. As I said before, that's how my mom and I made everything when I was a kid. And sometimes, for smaller batches of something, a hand mixer is better than a big stand mixer. As much as I love my stand mixer, if I don't put enough in that big bowl, the bottom just doesn't get mixed. Invest in a good hand mixer; you want it to last a long time. Mine is Cuisinart, and it's still going thirteen years later.

Stand Mixer. This bad boy is the gold standard. It's expensive. Extravagant, even. But if you can, get one. It just gets the job done quicker. Batters and doughs come together in half the time that they do using a hand mixer. I make all my yeasted breads in my Kitchen Aid with no hand kneading because of the dough hook. A regular 5-quart bowl is good for the average home cook.

BIG Food Processor. This is one of those items I didn't know I needed until I had one. When we got married, I got a small food processor that turned into a blender. It was okay, but I barely ever used it, because it wasn't big enough. Just to make a batch of hummus I'd have to divide the recipe in two. One day I spent some birthday money on a 12-cup Cuisinart, and I never looked back. You can do so much in a food processor, from chopping nuts and crushing cookies for crusts to making nut butters (see the Oreo Peanut Butter, page 111) and pastry crust. I make all my pie crusts in my food processor. And it's amazingly easy!

Electric Griddle. Now, this is totally not necessary, it's just something I love. Of course, it's great for pancakes and grilled cheese, but did you know that a griddle heated on its lowest setting (usually about 200°F) is perfect for keeping chocolate warm while you're dipping truffles? That's a must if it's cold outside! (See page 30 for Candy Dipping Tips.)

Ingredient Tips and Substitutions

When I'm writing a recipe, I always try to think of the busy mom who needs to make this dessert for some function and doesn't have a ton of time (or money) to spend making it. Now, of course, not every recipe falls into this category, but I always try to cater to that baker because, well, I'm her. I'm a stay-at-home mom, a wife, and I have a full-time, work-at-home job. Sure, I'm baking all day for my job, but I still want it to be easy, fun, and affordable.

I would love to say I shop exclusively at a high-end grocery store and buy only organic products, but I'd be lying. I shop almost exclusively at Walmart and my local grocery store. I love store brands, although I do have a particular affinity for some name brands, and I'm loyal to those because I know how their products perform.

Let's talk a little bit about some of the key ingredients you'll find in this book, and substitutions you can make if you need to.

Butter. The recipes in this book were all created using unsalted butter. Unsalted butter lets you control the amount of salt going into your recipe. If you happen to only have salted butter on hand, you can use it, but you should adjust the amount of salt called for in the recipe. You can reduce the salt by $1/4$ teaspoon for each $1/2$ cup of salted butter that is substituted for unsalted. Another butter tip: If you're like me and forget to leave it out to soften before baking, you can microwave it. Start at 10 seconds on high, then turn it over and heat in 5-second increments until it's soft but not melted (for an 1100-watt microwave).

Sugar. This book uses three kinds of sugars: granulated, light brown, and powdered. Granulated and powdered sugars should not be packed into a measuring cup, but measured in level scoops. Brown sugar is always packed (scoop it into the measuring cup and press it down with your palm to pack it).

Vanilla Extract. As much as I love good vanilla, I go through a lot of it. Unless I want to mortgage my house to buy it, I have to purchase the large bottles from Costco. Whatever you buy, please make sure that it's pure vanilla extract. Save money by buying the generic brand, but don't buy the imitation vanilla. (And if you want a splurge, try vanilla bean paste. It's got amazing flavor and adds flecks of vanilla beans to your desserts.)

Flour. All of the recipes in this book use all-purpose flour. It's my go-to flour. Be sure not to pack your flour. The general rule of thumb is that flour should be spooned into the measuring cup, then leveled.

Peanut Butter. As you look at the recipes in this book, you'll realize how much I love peanut butter. I'm addicted to all kinds: creamy, crunchy, natural, regular . . . the list goes on. For baking, I stick with no-stir, mainstream brands because they're so predictable. My brand of choice is Skippy's Naturals, which is a no-stir salted peanut butter. Sometimes crunchy or creamy matters, but often it doesn't, so check the ingredient lists of the recipes carefully.

Cocoa Powder. Lots of recipes in this book use cocoa powder, most often the traditional unsweetened cocoa powder that you can find in the regular grocery store. I love the Hershey's brand. They also make a Special Dark cocoa powder, which is a cross between the regular unsweetened and a Dutch process cocoa. This Special Dark adds amazing flavor to chocolate desserts and can be substituted in many recipes.

Chocolate. You'll notice that many of my recipes (especially brownies) call for ounces of baking chocolate. There are many different kinds and cacao levels of baking chocolate, but the ones I use in these recipes are semisweet and unsweetened. My two favorite brands are the ones you find in regular grocery stores: Ghirardelli and Baker's. Using these chocolates adds a depth of flavor to recipes, more than just cocoa powder can give them. Baking chocolate like this can also be used for dipping truffles and candy in lieu of the melting chocolate called for in the recipes. (See Candy Dipping Tips, page 30.)

Chocolate Chips. All chocolate chips are not created equal. If you've ever done a taste test between store-brand chips and name-brand ones, you'll know that. This is one area I like to splurge a little. My favorite brands are Ghirardelli, Guittard, and Hershey's. You'll notice that many recipes call for mini chocolate chips. These are mainly a Nestle product (semisweet), but I've also seen them sold by Guittard. Sometimes you just need a mini chocolate chip, and I love using them in lots of different ways.

Sweetened Condensed Milk. I'm addicted to the stuff. If someone bet me to, I would probably drink it. It's great in so many recipes! You'll notice that I always use fat-free sweetened condensed milk. I know that seems like an oxymoron, but it's what I love. Different brands might perform a little differently, or be a little thicker (or thinner) than others, but for the most part you're safe using generic or regular. The main brand, Eagle, sells both regular and fat-free versions, as does the Walmart brand.

Cream Cheese. This is pretty straightforward, although many brands perform differently than others. I prefer the Philadelphia brand, but I do occasionally use generic, so you're safe both ways. Most of the recipes in this book call for full-fat, but you can often get away with substituting low-fat, except in cheesecakes. Fat-free should not be substituted for full-fat. You will not get good results with fat-free cream cheese. Just like butter, you can soften cream cheese in the microwave if you forget to let it sit out. Be sure to remove the wrapper and then heat it in 15 to 20–second increments on high until it's soft enough to use in your recipe.

Pie Crust. Okay, so let's talk about pie crust for just a second, okay? You can find my favorite All-Butter Pie Crust on page 64, and it's my go-to recipe. But I do, on occasion, use a store-bought crust. In that case I recommend the name brand Pillsbury because their product performs better than any other I've tried, and believe me, I've tried them all.

Cooking Spray. You'll see that almost all my recipes include cooking spray to grease the pans. I always line my pans with foil and spray them with the spray. You can use the store or name brand; I don't find much difference between them. You're welcome to use butter or shortening to grease your pans, but I just love the ease of the spray. I usually use a vegetable oil or the butter-flavored one for most recipes, and when indicated, I also occasionally use the kind with flour.

Milk, Buttermilk, and Cream. Many of the recipes in this book call for milk, buttermilk, or heavy whipping cream. Unless otherwise stated, anything calling for milk means whole milk. I don't like to substitute low- or nonfat milk for whole milk very often in baking, because lots of desserts (especially cakes) need the fat to stay nice and moist. Sometimes the substitution works, and sometimes it doesn't, so be sure to use what's called for.

Buttermilk is one of those enigmas that I can bet you don't use very often. It's something you put on your grocery list so you can make a recipe but forget to buy because by the time you get to the milk aisle you're on autopilot and just want to get home. If you forget to bring home the buttermilk, you can make your own by mixing 1 tablespoon of vinegar or lemon juice and enough milk to make 1 cup. Let it sit for 5 minutes, then use as directed.

Heavy whipping cream is another one of those perplexing ingredients. You go to the store and they sell whipping cream and heavy whipping cream and you instantly forget which one to buy. All the recipes that call for it in this book use heavy whipping cream. Heavy whipping cream has a slightly higher fat content, and it's able to stand up better in frostings and whipped cream. Try to remember: You want it heavy!

Eggs. I went through so many eggs writing this book I lost track. All of the recipes use large eggs. You can buy whatever brand you like, just make sure to get large ones.

Storage and Freezing Tips

Sometimes you feel like one cupcake, not a dozen. Or your family eats 10 cookies, not 36. This is a problem I have often, because I bake so much. You can only eat so much dessert! Want a dirty little secret? I freeze pretty much everything. I hate throwing away food, so the freezer in my garage is stocked for the next dessert shortage.

Here are some tips and tricks I've found for dealing with leftover desserts:

Cookies and Bars. You can freeze most cookies and bars easily. Place them between layers of paper towels in a resealable container or gallon-size bag. Freeze flat. When you're ready to eat them, let them defrost at room temperature, leaving the paper towels between the layers to absorb extra moisture. This is a great way to make holiday platters ahead of time or prep for a party a few days (or weeks) in advance. Most cookies and bars taste good even a month or two after freezing.

Cupcakes and Cakes. These are harder to freeze, but it can be done. While you can freeze a fully frosted cake or cupcakes, it's best to plan ahead. If you're making a recipe for future use, bake the cupcakes and let them cool completely. Place them on a cookie sheet and freeze for about 1 hour, then transfer to a gallon-size resealable bag. This way they won't stick together. The paper towel tip works here as well.

Cakes should be wrapped in two layers of plastic wrap and placed in a resealable bag prior to freezing (once they're cool). Let defrost at room temperature and don't use the microwave. Frostings can be place in resealable bags or containers and frozen as well. Stir thawed frosting with a spoon or spatula and if it's too thick for spreading, you can add a little milk or cream to make it spreadable. Just use your judgment.

Pie. If wrapped well (two layers of plastic wrap) and placed in a resealable container, most pies (except custard-based ones) can be frozen. I have successfully frozen chess pies, brownie pies, and nut pies. If you're dealing with leftover pie that doesn't have whipped cream all over it, I love to cut slices and place them in resealable sandwich bags for freezing. These become the best single-serve desserts when you're craving pie!

Cheesecake. I deal with cheesecake the same way I deal with pie. I've had success freezing slices, as well as whole cheesecakes, in plastic bags. Cheesecake bars can be frozen like you freeze blondies and brownies, between paper towels in resealable bags.

Candy. Yep, I freeze that too. I like to freeze truffles, fudge, and other candies in a single layer on a waxed paper–lined cookie sheet. Once frozen, I place them in resealable bags and pop them back in the freezer. They usually defrost okay, although dipped candies might lose their luster a little bit.

Breakfast but Better

Breakfast can be pretty boring in my house. We're often rushing out the door to school, the gym, or starting our workday, so breakfast ends up being some cereal or a smoothie. But sometimes? Sometimes I want a totally indulgent breakfast, and not just on a holiday. That's where the weekend comes in! These recipes are perfect for that lazy Saturday, a Sunday brunch, or just because you need a little comfort start to your day.

Carrot Cake Coffee Cake

Yield 8 to 12 servings   **Prep Time** 25 minutes   **Bake Time** 35 minutes

Carrot cake is one of the only treats my husband eats, and he loves this mash-up version of it!

Make the Cake

1. Preheat the oven to 350°F. Spray a 9-inch round pan with cooking spray.

2. Whisk the flour, baking powder, salt, and cinnamon together in a medium bowl.

3. Stir together the sugar, oil, and egg in a large bowl until the egg is thoroughly mixed in and all ingredients are combined. Stir in the milk. Stir the dry ingredients into the wet until just combined. Stir in the shredded carrots.

4. Pour the batter into the prepared pan.

Make the Streusel

1. Stir together the brown sugar, flour, cinnamon, and butter. Add the walnuts, if using.

2. Sprinkle the streusel on top of the batter in the pan. Bake for 25 to 35 minutes, until a toothpick inserted 2 inches from the edge of the pan comes out clean. Cool completely in the pan before frosting.

Make the Icing

1. In a medium bowl, beat the butter and cream cheese together with a hand mixer until smooth. Slowly mix in the powdered sugar, then beat in the vanilla.

2. Frost the top of the coffee cake, or serve the frosting on the side so guests can add their own.

3. Store the cake loosely covered with plastic wrap. It will keep for 2 to 3 days at room temperature.

Cake

1½ cups all-purpose flour

2 teaspoons baking powder

½ teaspoon salt

1 teaspoon ground cinnamon

¾ cup granulated sugar

¼ cup vegetable oil

1 large egg

½ cup whole milk

2 cups shredded carrots (about 4 carrots)

Streusel

½ cup packed brown sugar

2 tablespoons all-purpose flour

2 teaspoons ground cinnamon

2 tablespoons unsalted butter, melted

¾ cup chopped walnuts (optional)

Icing

1 tablespoon unsalted butter

2 ounces cream cheese

¾ cup powdered sugar

½ teaspoon vanilla extract

Tip This can also be baked in a 9-inch square pan.

Chocolate Chip Monkey Bread Muffins

Yield 12 muffins **Active Time** 25 minutes **Rising Time** 4 hours or overnight **Bake Time** 18 minutes

Monkey bread started as a Christmas morning staple in our house. It's my daughter's favorite breakfast, and now she asks for it all year long. These muffins are something you can make ahead and freeze for serving on those days your kids (or you!) are just craving monkey bread.

Make the Dough

1. Place the milk in a microwave-safe measuring cup. Heat in the microwave on high, until it's about 110°F (30 to 60 seconds, depending on your microwave). Add the yeast and stir. Let it sit for a few minutes, until the yeast blooms.

2. Place the sugar, butter, salt, and egg in the bowl of a stand mixer fitted with the paddle attachment. Mix until the butter is distributed throughout the liquids, although it may be chunky. Pour in the milk mixture and stir for a few seconds.

3. Add the flour and stir just until the mixture starts to stick to the paddle. Add the mini chocolate chips. Then replace the paddle with the dough hook. Continue mixing on medium speed until the dough forms a ball in the center of the bowl.

4. Spray a large bowl with cooking spray and place the dough ball in it. Lightly spray the top of the dough ball with cooking spray and cover the bowl with plastic wrap. Let sit for 4 hours in a warm, draft-free place until it doubles in size, or place in the refrigerator overnight.

(continued on next page)

Dough

¾ cup nonfat milk

1 package active dry yeast (about 2¼ teaspoons)

⅓ cup granulated sugar

3 tablespoons unsalted butter, softened

½ teaspoon salt

1 large egg

3 cups all-purpose flour, plus more for dusting

1 cup semisweet mini chocolate chips

Assembly

⅓ cup granulated sugar

1 teaspoon ground cinnamon

6 tablespoons (¾ stick) unsalted butter

¼ cup packed brown sugar

Assemble the Monkey Bread

1. If the dough has been in the refrigerator, let it sit at room temperature for 15 minutes.

2. Preheat the oven to 350°F. Spray the cavities and entire top of a 12-cup muffin pan with cooking spray.

3. Turn out the dough onto a cutting board dusted lightly with flour. Divide the dough into 48 pieces.

4. Stir together the granulated sugar and cinnamon for the rolling mixture in a small bowl. Roll each piece of dough in the mixture to coat.

5. Melt the butter for the topping in a microwave-safe bowl. Whisk in the brown sugar. Place 1 to 2 teaspoons of topping in the bottom of each muffin cup. Place 4 monkey bread dough pieces in each. Divide any remaining topping over the top.

6. Place the muffin pan on a cookie sheet to catch any overflow. Bake for 15 to 18 minutes, until browned. The topping will cook over onto the top of the muffin pan, but if it is sprayed well, it will clean up easily. Cool slightly before serving. Store in a sealed container. The muffins will keep for 2 to 3 days at room temperature.

Tip You can bake the muffins as one large monkey bread in a 12-cup Bundt pan. Baking time will be longer.

Sconuts
(aka Scone Doughnuts)

Yield 8 sconuts   **Prep Time** 30 minutes   **Cook Time** 35 minutes

This is the ultimate two-in-one breakfast: a scone fried like a doughnut. I thought I loved scones made the regular way, but that's before I'd ever had a sconut. I cannot get enough of them! They're light and fluffy inside, the way I love a scone to be, and the frying gives them a crunchy exterior that so complements all three of the toppings. Next time you feel like indulging in a doughnut, make a sconut instead!

Make the Sconuts

1. Pour the oil in a heavy-bottomed pot to a depth of 2 inches. Begin heating the oil to 350°F over medium heat. Cover a cookie sheet with paper towels. (Be sure to watch the oil temperature as you are making the sconuts so it does not get too hot. It's best to use a heavy-bottomed pot so it's easier to regulate the oil temperature. Leave a candy thermometer in the pot of oil while you're cooking so you can be sure the temperature stays close to 350°F. If the temperature starts to get too hot or drop too low, adjust the burner lower or higher to regulate it.)

2. Place the flour, sugar, baking powder, and salt in a food processor. Pulse once or twice to combine. Add the butter and pulse a few times, until distributed. Add the vanilla and milk to the food processor and process until the dough comes together in a ball.

3. Turn out the ball of dough onto a cutting board that's been lightly dusted with flour. Form the dough into a circle that is 5 to 6 in diameter and about ½-inch thick. Slice into 8 wedges.

Note You'll need a candy or frying thermometer for this recipe, unless you're a pro at frying!

Sconuts

About 6 cups vegetable oil, for frying

1 cup all-purpose flour, plus more for dusting

¼ cup granulated sugar

1 teaspoon baking powder

¼ teaspoon salt

3 tablespoons cold unsalted butter, diced

1 teaspoon vanilla extract

¼ cup whole milk

Cinnamon-Sugar Topping

½ cup granulated sugar

2 teaspoons ground cinnamon

(continued on next page)

Chocolate Glaze

¾ cup semisweet or milk chocolate chips (semisweet or milk)

3 tablespoons light corn syrup

3 tablespoons heavy whipping cream

Maple Glaze

1 cup powdered sugar

1 tablespoon whole milk

1 tablespoon maple syrup

¼ teaspoon maple extract (optional)

4. Check to make sure the oil is at 350°F. Cook just 1 or 2 scones at a time. Drop each into the hot oil and cook for 2 to 3 minutes, until they are a dark golden brown. Halfway through cooking, carefully flip the scnouts with a spoon. Remove the scnouts from the oil with a slotted spoon and place on the paper towel–lined cookie sheet. Let cool before glazing or dipping in one of the toppings. Store in a sealed container at room temperature; best eaten within 2 days.

Make the Cinnamon-Sugar Topping

1. Stir together the sugar and cinnamon in a wide bowl. Let the scnouts cool for 5 minutes, then dip and gently roll each one in the cinnamon-sugar.

Make the Chocolate Glaze

1. Let the scones cool completely before glazing. Heat the chocolate chips and corn syrup in a microwave-safe bowl for 30 seconds on high. Stir to combine. Add the heavy whipping cream and whisk until smooth. Dip the top of each scone in the glaze, and let sit to harden.

Make the Maple Glaze

1. Let the scones cool completely before glazing. Whisk together all the glaze ingredients in a small bowl. Dip the top of each scone in the maple glaze and refrigerate to set. Dip a second time for a thicker glaze, if desired.

Tip You can also use a stand mixer to make the scnout dough, but I don't recommend mixing them by hand or with a hand mixer as you might make a normal scone. The dough needs to be completely mixed (like a sugar cookie dough) so the scones don't fall apart when frying.

Blueberry Muffin Waffles

Yield 6 (7-inch) waffles **Prep Time** 15 minutes **Cook Time** 15 minutes

My mom has an amazing blueberry muffin recipe. I remember waking up on Saturday mornings and hearing her clattering around in the kitchen making them for breakfast. These waffles are the best of my mom's blueberry muffins, made in a waffle iron. They're Saturday morning muffins, but you can serve them with syrup!

Make the Waffles

1. Preheat a waffle iron to medium-high heat.

2. In a large bowl, whisk together the oil, milk, and eggs. Stir in the sugar. Add the flour and baking powder and stir until no lumps remain. Fold in the blueberries.

3. Spray the hot waffle iron with cooking spray. Fill the waffle iron with about ¾ cup of batter and cook until golden, 2 to 3 minutes. Carefully wipe off any blueberries that have stuck to the iron in between making each waffle. Repeat until all the batter is gone. Serve with butter and blueberry syrup. Store in a sealed container in the refrigerator; best eaten within 2 to 3 days. These also freeze well.

Make the Blueberry Syrup

1. Place all the ingredients in a small saucepan over medium-low heat. Bring to a boil. Gently mash the blueberries. Let boil for 2 minutes. Strain into a heat-safe syrup container and let cool. Store in the refrigerator.

Tip For a tasty variation, leave out the blueberries and use chocolate chips instead!

Waffles

½ cup vegetable oil

1 cup whole milk

2 large eggs

1 cup granulated sugar

1¾ cups all-purpose flour

1 teaspoon baking powder

1 cup blueberries (fresh or frozen and defrosted)

Blueberry Syrup

1 cup blueberries (fresh or frozen and defrosted)

1 tablespoon lemon juice

½ cup pure maple syrup

Overnight Pumpkin Cheesecake French Toast

Yield 8–10 servings   **Active Time** 20 minutes   **Inactive Time** 8 to 12 hours   **Cook Time** 45 minutes

If you've never made overnight French toast, you're in for a morning treat! This is one of those breakfasts you can make after dinner and just pop in the oven the next morning, which is perfect if you love pumpkin but you're not a morning person. It's pumpkin squared in this breakfast: pumpkin cheesecake–filled bread and pumpkin in the egg mixture. Who says pumpkin is only for fall? We love it all year long!

Make the Pumpkin Cheesecake

1. With an electric hand mixer, beat the cream cheese and 2 tablespoons pumpkin puree until smooth. Mix in the brown sugar, graham cracker crumbs, and pumpkin pie spice.

2. Cut the bread into ¹/₂-inch slices. Make sandwiches with the pumpkin cream cheese mixture. Cut each sandwich into large bite-size pieces (4 to 6 pieces per sandwich). Spray a 9 x 13-inch baking dish with cooking spray, and place the sandwich pieces in the dish.

Make the Egg Mixture

1. Whisk the eggs in a large bowl. Add the pumpkin puree and ¹/₃ cup brown sugar. Whisk in the pumpkin pie spice, vanilla, salt, and milk. Pour over the bread in the baking dish. Press lightly down with your hands to coat all the bread with the egg mixture.

2. Cover with plastic wrap and refrigerate for 8 hours or overnight.

(continued on next page)

Pumpkin Cheesecake

3 ounces cream cheese, room temperature

2 tablespoons pumpkin puree

¼ cup packed brown sugar

¼ cup graham cracker crumbs (1 to 2 whole graham crackers)

1 teaspoon pumpkin pie spice

16 ounces (1 pound) day-old French bread

Egg Mixture

4 large eggs

½ cup pumpkin puree

¹/₃ cup packed brown sugar

2 teaspoons pumpkin pie spice

1 teaspoon vanilla extract

½ teaspoon salt

2 cups whole milk

Bake the French Toast

1. Preheat the oven to 350°F. Remove the pan from the refrigerator and remove plastic wrap. Press down to coat the top with the egg mixture that hasn't soaked in. Bake for 35 to 45 minutes, until set and hot in the middle.

2. Cool slightly before serving. Serve with maple syrup. Store covered with plastic wrap in the refrigerator; best eaten within two days.

Tip Substitute mashed banana for the pumpkin for a whole new breakfast!

Candy Concoctions

Although I love making candy all year long, I especially crave it during the holiday months. One of my favorite things to give for Christmas and Valentine's Day are little tins of candy. From truffles to bark to fudge, this chapter is super sweet. The recipes are wonderful for the holidays, but your family will beg for them all year long!

Candy Dipping Tips

Afew of the recipes in this section talk about dipping things in chocolate. If you've never done that before, it can be daunting and sometimes even frustrating. Don't fret! Dipping can be easy, especially with practice. Nothing is ever perfect on the first try . . . and sometimes not even on the tenth. I've been doing this for years, and even now I sometimes look at my truffles and wonder how a round sphere turned into the shape of a brain.

Here are some tips and tricks to make dipping much easier:
Use a chocolate meant for dipping. As easy as it is to grab a bag of chocolate chips instead of buying a melting chocolate, the results just aren't the same. And while I love using semisweet chocolate baking squares for dipping, sometimes you need something a little more stable and less likely to seize. Chocolate, especially white chocolate, can be very finicky when you're dipping. One wrong move and it seizes, and you have to start over, which is a really big waste of money. That's when chocolate made especially for melting comes in handy. There are a few brands out there, and they all have their pros and cons. The three most recognizable brands are Almond Bark (Plymouth Pantry), Wilton Candy Melts, and Candiquik. Almond Bark is the cheapest and can be found in most grocery stores at the holidays and at Walmart year round. It's a good product, but it's my least favorite, flavor-wise. Wilton is the most readily available if you

live near a craft store (like Michael's or Joann Fabrics). They come in all sorts of colors and flavors, melt really well, and taste good. But my favorite of the three is Candiquik. It can be harder to find, but some grocery stores and usually Target and Walmart carry it. Candiquik has the best flavor, but it's also the most expensive. Try what you can find, and pick your favorite.

Semisweet chocolate baking squares (such as Baker's or Ghirardelli) are also good for dipping. Make sure the chocolate is chopped fine and melted either over a double boiler or in 30-second increments in the microwave, stirring between each one. Adding 1 teaspoon of shortening per 4-ounce bar will help the chocolate melt smooth.

Use a griddle to keep your chocolate warm. The worst thing about dipping is when you get clumpy chocolate, and that's going to happen after a while as the chocolate cools. I use an electric griddle set at its lowest temperature (about 200°F) and I line it with a couple of kitchen towels. My chocolate sits in a bowl on top, and the heat from the griddle keeps it melted. If you don't have a griddle, you can use a double boiler (or a bowl over a pan of boiling water; just make sure the bowl doesn't actually touch the water).

Use the right bowl. If you're melting chocolate in the microwave for dipping, you need to use

  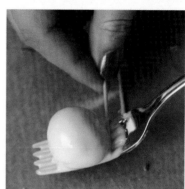

the right bowl. I don't like using glass bowls because they can get too hot and seize the chocolate. My favorite kind is a sturdy plastic bowl (not the throwaway kind). It's sturdy enough for the microwave and won't get too hot on the griddle.

Drop your candy in the bowl of chocolate but do not swirl it. Spoon the chocolate over the top instead. This will reduce the chances of the candy crumbling into the chocolate.

Use a fork to lift the candy out of the bowl. The excess chocolate can drip through the tines of the fork. Don't tap the fork on the bowl, and

don't tap the fork with your fingers. Instead, tap the back of the hand holding the fork. This reduces the shake so your candy will stay on the fork. Swipe it along the edge of the bowl to help remove excess chocolate.

Use a toothpick to help you transfer the truffle or candy from the fork to the cookie sheet. The toothpick helps the candy slide off the fork with minimal disruption to the melted chocolate.

Sprinkles hide a lot of imperfections! Why do you think my truffles are always bathed in sprinkles?

Lemon Meringue Pie Fudge

Yield 36 pieces   **Prep Time** 5 minutes   **Bake Time** 10 minutes   **Chill Time** 4 to 6 hours

Making pie into fudge is one of my favorite mash-ups. Anytime I can add a crust to a recipe is a happy day! I love that this fudge has the elements of lemon meringue pie, but it's bite-size. Cutting my pie-inspired fudges into triangles for serving, to look like little slices of pie, is one of my favorite things to do!

Make the Crust

1. Preheat the oven to 350°F and spray an 8 x 8-inch pan with cooking spray or line with foil and spray with cooking spray for easy cleanup.

2. In a medium bowl, mix the cookie crumbs and melted butter, and press into the prepared pan. Bake for 10 minutes. Let cool while you prepare the filling.

Make the Lemon Meringue Fudge

1. Place the white chocolate chips in a medium saucepan. Add the sweetened condensed milk and warm over medium-low heat, stirring, until melted.

2. Once the mixture in the pan has melted, remove from the heat and stir in the lemon extract, lemon zest, and food coloring, if using. Pour two-thirds of the fudge over the crust and spread. Working quickly, add the marshmallow fluff to the remaining fudge in the saucepan. Fold, being careful to not totally mix them together; you want swirls of fudge and fluff. Pour and spread over the fudge already in pan.

3. Let cool to room temperature and then refrigerate to set. Slice into squares or triangles and serve. Cover and store at room temperature or in the refrigerator. The fudge will for keep 3 to 4 days.

Crust

1¾ cups shortbread cookie crumbs

¼ cup (½ stick) unsalted butter, melted

Lemon Meringue Fudge

3 cups white chocolate chips

1 (14-ounce) can fat-free sweetened condensed milk

1 teaspoon pure lemon extract

1 teaspoon grated lemon zest

2 to 3 drops yellow food coloring (optional)

1 cup marshmallow fluff

Tip Making fudge is one of those things that goes really fast. Have all your ingredients ready to go near the stove. Get the lemon extract, food coloring, and lemon zest ready to add, and measure out your marshmallow fluff before you begin melting the chocolate.

Mint Chip Truffles

Yield 18 truffles **Prep Time** 30 minutes **Chill Time** 1 hour

This recipe is for my daughter, Jordan. She is a mint-chip addict! No matter what, when I ask her what treats I should make or what birthday cake she wants, she asks for chocolate and mint. These candies are buttercream truffles that taste like mint-chip ice cream. She proclaimed them, "Fabulicious with a side of blingy ding ding awesome!" and I hope you feel the same way.

1. In a large bowl, mix the butter and powdered sugar with a hand mixer until crumbly. Add the vanilla and peppermint extracts and salt, then mix until smooth. It will seem like it takes forever, but it will happen after a few minutes. Depending on your hand mixer, you can turn it up to medium or medium-high speed and the mixture will come together faster.

2. Once smooth, mix in the green food coloring on low speed. Then stir in the mini chocolate chips. Refrigerate for 30 minutes.

3. Scoop 1-tablespoon balls of cold dough and place them on a waxed paper–lined cookie sheet. Refrigerate for at least another 30 minutes.

4. When you're ready to dip the truffles, melt the melting chocolate or semisweet baking chocolate according to the package directions and line a cookie sheet with waxed paper. Remove the truffles from refrigerator and roll into smooth balls. These soften pretty quickly, so it's best to keep them in the refrigerator and only remove 4 or 5 at a time to dip.

5. Dip each truffle in the melted chocolate (see Candy Dipping Tips, page 30), tapping off any excess, and place them on the prepared cookie sheet. Sprinkle with sprinkles, if using. Return to the refrigerator to harden. Store in an airtight container in the refrigerator; they soften quickly. The truffles will keep for several days when kept cold.

½ cup (1 stick) unsalted butter, at room temperature

1½ cups powdered sugar

1 teaspoon vanilla extract

⅛ teaspoon peppermint extract

¼ teaspoon salt

2 drops green food coloring

¼ cup semisweet mini chocolate chips

8 ounces melting chocolate or semisweet baking chocolate

Sprinkles (optional)

Tip Be sure to buy peppermint extract not mint extract. They are two very different flavors, so be sure to check the box!

Cheesecake Chocolate Chip Cookie Dough Truffles

Yield About 38 truffles **Prep Time** 30 minutes **Active Time** 1 hour **Chill Time** About 2 hours

These truffles take a little work, but they are the ultimate indulgence. I discovered my love of cheesecake truffles a few years ago, and I cannot get enough of those delicious bites. Sandwiched between layers of eggless chocolate chip cookie dough, cheesecake is taken to a whole new level!

Make the Cheesecake

1. Beat the cream cheese, sugar, vanilla, and graham cracker crumbs in a large bowl using a hand mixer. Refrigerate for 30 minutes.

2. Once the cheesecake mixture is cold, scoop 1-tablespoon balls onto a waxed paper–lined cookie sheet. (You will get about 22 cheesecake balls using a 1-tablespoon cookie scoop.) Cut each ball in half, for a total of about 44 balls. Freeze for at least 15 minutes.

Make the Chocolate Chip Cookie Dough

1. In the bowl of a stand mixer fitted with the paddle attachment, cream together the butter, brown sugar, and granulated sugar. Mix in the vanilla, milk, and salt. Slowly add the flour and mix on low until incorporated. Stir in the mini chocolate chips. Scoop 1-tablespoon balls onto a waxed paper–lined cookie sheet. (You will get about 38 cookie balls using a 1-tablespoon cookie scoop.) Refrigerate for 30 minutes.

(continued on next page)

Cheesecake

8 ounces (1 package) cream cheese, at room temperature

¼ cup granulated sugar

¼ teaspoon vanilla extract

½ cup graham cracker crumbs (from 2 whole graham crackers)

Chocolate Chip Cookie Dough

¾ cup (1½ sticks) unsalted butter, at room temperature

¾ cup packed brown sugar

½ cup granulated sugar

1½ teaspoons pure vanilla extract

1 tablespoon whole milk

¼ teaspoon salt

1½ cups all-purpose flour

¾ cup semisweet mini chocolate chips

16 ounces melting chocolate or semisweet baking chocolate

Extra graham cracker crumbs or sprinkles, for garnish

(continued on next page)

Assemble the Truffles

1. Flatten each cold cookie dough ball with the palm of your hand. Place a cheesecake truffle in the center of each cookie dough round and wrap it around the cheesecake. Roll between your hands to seal and form a large ball. It's okay if the cheesecake pokes through a little. Repeat until all truffles have been made. Refrigerate again, for at least 15 minutes. (They can also be covered with plastic wrap and refrigerated overnight.) You will have about 38 truffles, with a few cheesecake balls left over. Discard the extra cheesecake . . . or eat it!

2. Melt the chocolate in a microwave-safe bowl according to the package directions and line a cookie sheet with waxed paper. Dip each truffle into the chocolate and coat completely (see Candy Dipping Tips page 30). Tap off the excess and set onto the prepared cookie sheet. Sprinkle with graham cracker crumbs or sprinkles. Refrigerate to set. Store in an airtight container in the refrigerator. Truffles will keep for up to 5 days.

Tip You're not limited to chocolate chip cookie dough—you can use your favorite cookie dough recipe for these truffles. Just leave out the leavening and eggs in your recipe; you can substitute 1 tablespoon milk for each egg to help bind the mixture.

Peanut Butter Cup Brownie Bites

Yield 32 bites   Prep Time 1 hour   Bake Time 18 to 25 minutes   Chill Time 1 hour, plus cooling time

If I had to choose only one flavor combination to eat for the rest of my life, it would be peanut butter and chocolate. These bites are what happens when a peanut butter cup and a brownie get married and have babies: A layer of brownie is topped with a soft peanut butter mixture and then the whole thing takes a bath in chocolate. These are too easy to eat, so be sure to wrap some in a pretty box and give them to your neighbors . . . if you have the strength to share them!

Make the Brownies

1. Preheat the oven to 350°F. Spray a 9 x 9-inch pan with cooking spray or line with foil and spray with cooking spray for easy cleanup.

2. In a large bowl, stir together the melted butter, sugar, and cocoa. Stir in the eggs, vanilla, coffee (the coffee just adds a richness to the brownies, but you can use water if you prefer), and salt. Carefully stir in the flour. Spread in the prepared pan.

3. Bake for 18 to 25 minutes, until a toothpick inserted about 2 inches from the edge of the pan comes out with only crumbs sticking to it. Let cool completely in pan before continuing. You can chill them to speed up this process.

(continued on page 41)

Brownies

½ cup (1 stick) unsalted butter, melted

1 cup granulated sugar

⅔ cup unsweetened cocoa powder

2 large eggs

2 teaspoons vanilla extract

1 tablespoon brewed coffee (or water)

¼ teaspoon salt

½ cup all-purpose flour

Peanut Butter Mixture

1 cup creamy peanut butter

⅓ cup packed brown sugar

1 cup powdered sugar

1 teaspoon vanilla extract

16 to 24 ounces melting chocolate or semisweet baking chocolate

Sprinkles (optional)

Make the Peanut Butter Mixture

1. Combine the peanut butter, brown sugar, and powdered sugar in a large bowl. Mix with a hand mixer (or a stand mixer fitted with the paddle attachment) until crumbly. Add the vanilla, then continue to mix until the mixture is smooth and almost comes together. Press it together with your hands to form a smooth ball.

2. Place the peanut butter ball on a sheet of waxed paper. Press or roll it into a square that's about the size of your brownie pan. Place the peanut butter square on top of the brownies and press to adhere it. Press and adjust the edges so that it completely covers the brownies in the pan. Refrigerate for 30 minutes to 1 hour.

3. When you're ready to dip the brownies, melt half of the candy according to the package directions and line a cookie sheet with waxed paper. Remove the brownies from the pan and carefully discard the foil. Set the brownies on a cutting board and cut the square in half. Place one half back in the refrigerator until finished with the first half.

4. Cut the half sheet of brownies into 32 squares (4 rows by 8 columns). Dip each square carefully into the chocolate (see Candy Dipping Tips, page 30), tap off any excess, and place on the prepared cookie sheet. Repeat with the remaining brownies, melting additional chocolate as needed.

5. Refrigerate until set. If desired, place any remaining chocolate in a plastic baggie or small squirt bottle and drizzle chocolate on top of the truffles. You can also cover them with sprinkles or leave them plain. These can be kept at room temperature or in the refrigerator in an airtight container, or can be frozen. The truffles will keep for up to 5 days in the refrigerator.

Tip Use white candy coating for a fun new twist!

Chocolate Chip Cookie Toffee Bark

Yield About 8 cups   **Prep Time** 5 minutes   **Cook Time** 18 minutes   **Chill Time** 4 hours

Every year at Christmas I make some version of toffee bark using matzo crackers. It's the one thing everyone is addicted to, which is why it goes by the nickname "Christmas Crack." One day I wondered if I was limited to using crackers as a base, and I tried using store-bought crunchy chocolate chip cookies instead. In one bite my mind was blown, and I won't ever make cracker bark again . . . and neither will you!

30 crunchy chocolate chip cookies (such as Chips Ahoy)

1 cup (2 sticks) unsalted butter

1 cup packed brown sugar

1 tablespoon water

1 teaspoon vanilla extract

1 (11.5-ounce) bag semisweet or milk chocolate chips

1 cup toffee bits

1. Preheat the oven to 350°F. Line a 10 x 15-inch jelly roll pan or rimmed cookie sheet with foil and spray well with cooking spray. Arrange the cookies in a single layer in the pan, breaking a few to fill in the edges and gaps as much as possible.

2. Melt the butter in a saucepan over medium heat. Reduce the heat to medium-low and add the brown sugar and water. Bring to a boil, stirring occasionally. Once it boils, place the candy thermometer in the pan and do not stir. Let the mixture cook until it reaches 255°F on a candy thermometer, 5 to 7 minutes. Remove from the heat and stir in the vanilla. Immediately pour over the cookies and spread carefully to cover all the cookies. Bake for 5 minutes.

3. Remove the pan from the oven and sprinkle with the chocolate chips. Bake an additional 2 minutes. Remove the pan from the oven and, using an offset spatula, carefully spread the chocolate chips evenly over the toffee (they will have melted in the oven but still held their shape). Sprinkle the toffee chips over the chocolate. Let cool to room temperature, then refrigerate to set. Break into pieces and serve. Store at room temperature for up to 1 week.

Tip This supersweet bark is not limited to chocolate chip cookies—use your favorite crunchy cookie! Shortbread, peanut butter, chocolate, the options are endless.

Sugar Cookie Dough Cups

Yield 12 Prep Time 45 minutes Chill Time 1 hour 15 minutes

My father-in-law was a sugar-cookie fanatic. Every Christmas I'd make our family sugar cookies and I'd have to make him his own extra batch so he wouldn't eat all of ours (and he would have!). Over the years I started making lots of other sugar-cookie treats, from bars to candy, to give him for every holiday and birthday. I made these in his memory, and I know that he would have loved them (and eaten them all without gaining an ounce).

1. In the bowl of a stand mixer fitted with the paddle attachment or with a hand mixer in a large bowl, cream together the butter and sugar. Beat in the vanilla, milk, and flour.

2. Form the dough into a disk. Place between two sheets of waxed paper on a cutting board. Roll out to ¼ inch thick. I like to peel the waxed paper off the top, then flip the dough over and peel it off the bottom after every few rolls so that it doesn't stick. Refrigerate for at least 15 minutes.

3. Using a 2-inch round cookie cutter, cut 24 circles of dough, rerolling as necessary. Place half the dough rounds on top of the other half, for a total of 12. Refrigerate until ready to assemble cups.

4. Melt the melting chocolate according to the package directions. (See Candy Dipping Tips, page 30.)

5. Line a standard 12-cup muffin pan with paper liners. Spoon about 1 tablespoon of melting chocolate into the bottom of each liner, enough to coat the bottom. Tap the pan to settle the candy and release any air bubbles.

¼ cup (½ stick) unsalted butter, softened

½ cup granulated sugar

½ teaspoon vanilla extract

2 teaspoons whole milk

½ cup all-purpose flour

12 to 16 ounces vanilla-flavored melting chocolate

Sprinkles (optional)

(continued on next page)

6. Place one cookie dough round in each muffin liner. Top with 1 to 2 tablespoons more melting chocolate, spreading as necessary to make sure that the two edges of chocolate meet. Tap the pan again to release air bubbles. Top with sprinkles. Refrigerate until set, about 1 hour. Store in an airtight container in the refrigerator for up to one week. These can also be frozen.

Tip These are a big dose of sweet! To make them more bite-size, use a mini muffin pan, with mini muffin liners and a 1-inch round cookie cutter. You can also make these with your favorite flavor of cookie dough. Just substitute 1 tablespoon of milk for each egg called for in the recipe to make an eggless cookie dough, and you can omit any leavening that is called for. Use vanilla or chocolate candy melts, depending on your cookie dough flavor.

Cookies, Brownies, and Bars Together at Last!

It's hard for me to choose a favorite dessert (besides pie, of course), but if I had to, it would be a cookie, brownie, or bar. Good thing mash-ups mean you don't have to pick! There's something about the texture of a gooey cookie or a fudgy brownie that just screams comfort food. I love making batches of each and keeping them in the freezer for those times when I just need a sweet treat . . . and those times happen more often than I'd like to admit!

S'more Cookies

Yield 3 dozen cookies, about 18 large sandwiches   Prep Time 15 minutes
Chill Time 1 to 2 hours   Cook Time 10 minutes

S'mores are that quintessential summer campfire dessert. My problem? I don't camp. In fact, my family jokes that, for me, staying in a two-star hotel would be camping. Since I won't be pitching a tent in the great outdoors anytime soon, I like to come up with other ways to enjoy one of my favorite summer treats in the comfort of my air-conditioned house. These s'mores start with my favorite chocolate chip cookie recipe and have graham crackers added to the batter. The marshmallows are broiled to make them all melty between the cookies—perfect for you indoor s'more lovers! But, if you do love s'mores over the campfire, bake the cookies ahead of time and roast the marshmallows the old-fashioned way!

1 cup (2 sticks) unsalted butter, melted

¾ cup granulated sugar

1 cup packed brown sugar

2 large eggs

1 tablespoon vanilla extract

½ teaspoon salt

1 teaspoon baking soda

3¼ cups all-purpose flour

1¼ cups semisweet or milk chocolate chips

4 whole graham crackers, broken up into small bite-size pieces (just over 1 cup)

About 18 large marshmallows

1. Place the melted butter, granulated sugar, and brown sugar in the bowl of a stand mixer fitted with the paddle attachment. Mix until combined. Mix in the eggs and vanilla, then the salt and baking soda. With the mixer on low, add the flour, scraping down the sides of the bowl as needed. Stir in the chocolate chips and broken graham cracker pieces. (The graham crackers will break up even more in the mixing process, ensuring graham cracker in almost every bite!)

2. Refrigerate the dough for 1 to 2 hours. When ready to bake, preheat the oven to 350°F and line 2 cookie sheets with parchment paper or silicone baking mats.

3. Use a 2-tablespoon cookie scoop to drop balls of dough 2 inches apart on the cookie sheets. Flatten each one slightly with the palm of your hand.

(continued on page 50)

4. Bake for 9 to 12 minutes, until the cookies start to get golden on the bottom and they lose their sheen. (If you like your cookies on the softer, underdone side, about 10 minutes is perfect. Cook 11 to 12 minutes for a more done cookie.) Cool 5 minutes on the cookie sheet, then remove to a rack to cool completely.

5. To make s'mores, place half the cookies upside down on a parchment-lined cookie sheet. Set a large marshmallow on each cookie. Place under the broiler for just 30 to 60 seconds, until the marshmallows are toasty. Do not walk away from the oven—keep your eyes on them so they don't burn! Remove from the oven and sandwich with a second cookie. (You can also use a kitchen torch, if you have one, to toast the marshmallows, or actually grill the marshmallows on sticks over an open fire before adding them to the cookie sandwich.) Cookies can be stored in an airtight container for up to 4 days or frozen for up to 3 months. S'mores should be eaten immediately.

Tip Change up the s'mores flavor by using chocolate or cinnamon graham crackers, or even chocolate-covered graham cracker cookies!

Note These are large cookies. You can also make them with a smaller cookie scoop to end up with smaller sandwiches, but you will need to cut the large marshmallows in half so they fit on the cookie. Or you can use 2–3 mini marshmallows instead, depending on the cookie size.

Truffle-Topped Brownies

Yield 48 squares   **Prep Time** 15 minutes   **Cook Time** 23 minutes
Cool Time overnight

I am in love with brownies, but blogging spoiled me: I can no longer eat a regular, plain brownie. There needs to be some sort of frosting, topping, or stuffing inside. This recipe takes brownies to the next level, because they're not just frosted—they're topped with a rich and decadent truffle mixture. Chocolate truffles are so amazing, but they take so much time to roll. These brownies are a cinch to make and you just pour the truffle mixture over the top and let them harden before cutting.

Make the Brownies

1. Preheat the oven to 350°F. Spray a 9 x 13-inch pan with cooking spray or line with foil and spray with cooking spray for easy cleanup.

2. Place the two baking chocolates and butter in a large microwave-safe bowl. Heat on high power for 2 to 3 minutes, stirring every 30 seconds, until the chocolate is smooth. Stir in the sugar. Add the eggs, vanilla, and cocoa and stir well. Add the flour and salt, and stir carefully to combine.

3. Spread the batter in the prepared pan. Bake for 22 to 26 minutes, until a toothpick inserted 2 inches from edge of the pan comes out clean.

(continued on page 53)

Brownies

2 ounces unsweetened baking chocolate, coarsely chopped

2 ounces semisweet baking chocolate, coarsely chopped

¾ cup (1½ sticks) unsalted butter

1¾ cups granulated sugar

3 large eggs

1 tablespoon vanilla extract

2 tablespoons unsweetened cocoa powder

1 cup all-purpose flour

¼ teaspoon salt

Truffles

1½ cups heavy whipping cream

2 cups semisweet chocolate chips

Unsweetened cocoa powder or powdered sugar, for dusting

Make the Truffles

1. About 10 minutes before the brownies come out of the oven, combine the heavy whipping cream and chocolate chips in a large microwave-safe measuring cup or medium bowl. Heat for 1 minute in the microwave on high, then whisk. If the chocolate is not melted enough, heat in additional 30-second increments, whisking between each, until smooth.

2. When the brownies are finished baking, remove them from the oven. Pour the truffle mixture on top. Let cool to room temperature, then refrigerate overnight until set.

3. Dust the top of the set brownies with cocoa powder or powdered sugar. Slice into squares and serve. Store in the refrigerator, loosely covered, for up to 5 days.

Tip You can also top the brownies with toasted coconut or sprinkles for a different look to your truffle coating.

Cake Batter Blondie Bars

Yield 24 bars   **Prep Time** 25 minutes   **Bake Time** 22 minutes

Everyone loves sprinkles, including me. A jar of sprinkles can make my day! These bars are filled with sprinkles and cake batter flavor, without using a mix. The secret is in using butter extract. You'll be shocked at how much these bars taste like a slice of cake . . . but with the texture of a blondie!

Make the Blondie Bars

1. Preheat the oven to 350°F. Spray a 9 x 13-inch pan with cooking spray or line with foil and spray with cooking spray for easy cleanup.

2. In a medium bowl, whisk together the baking powder, salt, and flour. Set aside.

3. In the bowl of a stand mixer fitted with the paddle attachment, cream together the granulated sugar, brown sugar, and butter. Add the eggs, vanilla, and butter extract, and beat until combined. Add the dry ingredients and mix until combined. Stir in the sprinkles.

4. Press the dough into the prepared pan. (The dough will be sticky; spray your hands with cooking spray to keep it from sticking to you.) Bake for 22 to 24 minutes. They will be slightly golden, but still have the slightest jiggle in the center. They'll set as they cool. Cool completely before frosting.

Make the Frosting

1. Using an electric hand mixer or a stand mixer fitted with the paddle attachment, beat the butter until smooth. Slowly add in the powdered sugar and mix until crumbly. Add the vanilla, and milk and mix until smooth. Frost the bars. Top with sprinkles and cut into bars. Store covered at room temperature or in the refrigerator. Best eaten at room temperature within 5 days.

Blondie Bars

1 teaspoon baking powder

½ teaspoon salt

2 cups all-purpose flour

½ cup granulated sugar

1 cup packed brown sugar

½ cup (1 stick) unsalted butter, softened

2 large eggs

1 teaspoon vanilla extract

1 teaspoon butter extract

½ cup sprinkles

Frosting

½ cup (1 stick) unsalted butter, softened

1½ cups powdered sugar

1 teaspoon vanilla extract

1 teaspoon whole milk

Sprinkles, for garnish

Tip You can find butter extract at most grocery stores in the baking aisle.

Peanut Butter Brookies

Yield 24 bars   Prep Time 25 minutes   Bake Time 35 minutes

What happens when a brownie marries a cookie? They have brookie babies! This is my favorite brownie recipe on top of my favorite peanut butter cookie recipe. The result is one of those treats that makes people come back for seconds, thirds, and fourths. If you love peanut butter cookies and brownies, this is the recipe for you!

Peanut Butter Cookie Crust

1 cup creamy peanut butter

½ cup granulated sugar

½ cup packed brown sugar

1 large egg

Brownies

2 ounces unsweetened baking chocolate, coarsely chopped

2 ounces semisweet baking chocolate, coarsely chopped

¾ cup (1½ sticks) unsalted butter

1¾ cups sugar

3 large eggs

1 tablespoon vanilla extract

1 cup all-purpose flour

Make the Peanut Butter Cookie Crust

1. Preheat the oven to 350°F. Spray a 9 x 13-inch pan with cooking spray or line with foil and spray with cooking spray for easy cleanup.

2. Stir together the peanut butter, granulated sugar, brown sugar, and egg in a large bowl. Press into the bottom of the prepared pan. The dough will be thin. (It helps to spray your hands with cooking spray so the batter doesn't stick to you.)

Make the Brownies

1. Melt the two baking chocolates and the butter together in a large microwave-safe bowl. Microwave on high in 30-second increments, stirring between each, until the mixture is smooth. Stir in the sugar, then stir in the eggs and vanilla. Carefully stir in the flour. Pour the batter into the pan and carefully spread over the cookie crust.

2. Bake for 32 to 38 minutes, until the top is no longer glossy and is slightly cracked around the edges. Cool completely in pan, then slice into bars. Store in an airtight container for up to 5 days.

Rocky Road Cookie Fudge Bars

Yield 36 bars   **Prep Time** 20 minutes   **Bake Time** 18 minutes   **Chill Time** At least 4 hours

I'll never forget eating rocky road ice cream when I was young. It was one of my mom's favorite flavors, so it was always in the freezer. I'd pick out the almonds and marshmallows to save for last, because they were the best part. My love of the ice cream inspired these bars: a rich chocolate cookie bar topped with a rocky road candy that tastes like fudge. I hope it brings back memories of all your rocky road days like it does for me!

1. Preheat the oven to 350°F. Spray a 9 x 9-inch pan with cooking spray or line with foil and spray with cooking spray for easy cleanup.

2. In the bowl of a stand mixer fitted with the paddle attachment, cream together the butter, brown sugar, and granulated sugar. Add the vanilla and egg, and mix until smooth. Mix in the cocoa and baking soda, then add the salt and flour, and beat until well blended. Press into the prepared pan. (The batter will be sticky; it helps to spray your hands with cooking spray to keep it from sticking to you.)

3. Bake for 15 to 18 minutes, until the top just loses its sheen.

4. As soon as the bars come out of the oven (or a few minutes before), melt the chocolate chips in a large microwave-safe bowl on high for $1\frac{1}{2}$ to 2 minutes, stirring every 30 seconds until the chocolate melts and is smooth. Let it sit for about 2 minutes, then stir in the chopped nuts and mini marshmallows. Stir to coat completely.

5. Pour the marshmallow mixture on top of the hot cookie bars and spread carefully. Let set at room temperature before slicing. You can refrigerate the bars to speed hardening, but be sure to allow them to sit at room temperature for 30 minutes before slicing to avoid cracking in the chocolate. Store in an airtight container at room temperature; bars are best within 4 days.

½ cup (1 stick) unsalted butter, softened

½ cup packed brown sugar

¼ cup granulated sugar

1 teaspoon vanilla extract

1 large egg

⅓ cup unsweetened cocoa powder

1 teaspoon baking soda

¼ teaspoon salt

1 cup all-purpose flour

1 (11.5-ounce) bag semisweet or milk chocolate chips

½ cup chopped walnuts or almonds

1½ cups mini marshmallows

Cinnamon Roll Cookies

Yield 3 dozen cookies **Prep Time** 20 minutes **Chill Time** 1 hour **Bake Time** 10 minutes

If there is one food I cannot stop eating, it's a cinnamon roll. Seriously, don't leave me with a pan unattended or you'll come back to crumbs. I've turned cinnamon rolls into cake and crust before, but this is one of my favorite versions: a cookie. A sweet sugar cookie dough is rolled in a cinnamon-sugar filling and then sliced and baked. Topped with a sweet icing, these are the perfect way to enjoy a cinnamon roll . . . in a cookie!

Cookies

½ cup (1 stick) unsalted butter, softened

⅔ cup granulated sugar

½ cup packed brown sugar, divided

1 large egg

1 teaspoon vanilla extract

¼ teaspoon salt

2 cups all-purpose flour

2 teaspoons ground cinnamon

Frosting

1½ cups powdered sugar

1½ teaspoons vanilla extract

6 to 8 teaspoons whole milk

Make the Cookies

1. In the bowl of a stand mixer fitted with the paddle attachment, cream together the butter, granulated sugar, and ¼ cup of the brown sugar. Beat in the egg and vanilla. Add the salt and flour and beat until the dough just comes together.

2. Stir together the remaining ¼ cup brown sugar and the cinnamon in a small bowl. Set aside.

3. Divide the dough in half. Place a large sheet of waxed paper on a cutting board. Place half of the dough on the waxed paper and flatten slightly with your hands. Place a second layer of waxed paper over the top and roll into an 8-inch square. Remove the top sheet of waxed paper, sprinkle with half of the brown sugar–cinnamon mixture and roll up the dough. Repeat with second half of the dough. Cover with plastic wrap and refrigerate until firm, at least 1 hour.

4. Preheat the oven to 375°F. Line 2 cookie sheets with parchment paper or silicone baking mats.

5. Slice the dough logs into ¼ to ½-inch-thick cookies. Place cookies 2 inches apart on the prepared cookie sheets. Bake for 8 to 10 minutes, until the bottoms just start to turn golden brown. Cool 5 minutes on the cookie sheets before moving to a cooling rack. Let cool before frosting.

(continued on page 62)

Make the Frosting

1. Whisk the ingredients together in a medium bowl. Transfer the frosting to a plastic bag and cut off one tip. Pipe onto cookies. Chill to set frosting. Store in an airtight container for up to 4 days or freeze for up to 3 months.

Tip Add ½ teaspoon of maple extract to the frosting for a new flavor twist.

Pie Surprise

Well, you've probably guessed by now that pie is where my heart is. A big slice of pie is the ultimate comfort for me in so many ways. As much as I love a regular apple or chocolate pie, one of my favorite things to do is take non-pie flavors and turn them into my favorite dessert. From Chocolate Chip Cookies to Magic Bars and Milky Ways, these pies are two desserts...in one crust!

All-Butter Pie Crust

Yield 1 pie crust for a 9" pie   Prep Time 20 minutes   Chill Time 30 minutes

Everyone needs a good crust recipe in their repertoire, and for me, this is it. Opinions vary on fat in crust (shortening vs. lard vs. butter) and I love this All-Butter Pie Crust. What can I say? I love the flavor of butter and the delicateness it gives a crust. I call this crust a little rustic; it's not the prettiest girl in the room, but it's what's inside (and how it tastes) that counts!

This pie crust is great for filling and baking, and the recipe makes one crust that fits comfortably in a 9-inch pie plate. For a bigger pie plate or for a double crust, double the recipe.

2 to 3 tablespoons ice water

½ cup (1 stick) unsalted butter, diced and chilled

1¼ cups all-purpose flour

½ teaspoon salt

1. Fill a measuring cup or glass with ice and water.

2. Combine the flour and salt in a food processor. Pulse once to mix. Alternatively, whisk together in a large bowl.

3. If using a food processor, add the butter and process until it resembles coarse crumbs. Add 2 tablespoons of water and pulse for 15 to 20 seconds. If the dough starts to come together, let the processor run. If it's still very crumbly, add another tablespoon of water. You want the dough to form a ball that's not too wet. (I have found that the humidity in the air can affect how much water you add, so keep that in mind!) Turn out the dough onto a lightly floured surface.

4. Alternatively, without a food processor, cut in the butter using a pastry cutter. Work in 1 tablespoon of water at a time, then turn out the dough onto a floured surface. You're going to roll it out before you chill it. This makes it much easier to roll.

5. I recommend using a silicone baking mat or other similar silicone surface for rolling, but you don't have to; without one, you'll just have to use more flour. Press the dough ball into a disk and roll to about ¼ inch thick. Be sure to flip and rotate your dough as you go so it does not stick to your surface. Roll out the dough to a few inches larger than your pie plate (about 12 inches for a 9-inch pie plate).

6. Place the dough round in the pie plate and press to fit. Tuck under any overhang, and crimp or use the tines of a fork to decorate the edges. Cover with plastic wrap and refrigerate until ready to fill. For the top crust in a double-crust pie, roll out the dough and chill until the pie is filled and then top the pie as desired.

Tip When baking a pie with a crust like this, tear strips of foil about 2 inches wide, cut the strips in half, and wrap them around the edges of the crust. Bake the pie as directed, but remove the foil 15 to 20 minutes before the end of the baking time. This will help avoid an overdone, dry crust!

Chocolate Chip Cookie Pie

Yield 8 servings **Prep Time** 15 minutes plus the time to make the crust **Bake Time** 40 minutes

Have you ever had a chess pie? I'd never had one until I made a few last year, and man, it was love at first bite. A chess pie is made of eggs, butter, sugar, and often milk, and when it's baked it becomes smooth and creamy, like a not-quite-baked-through cookie. That's how this pie was born! I added some of my favorite cookie flavors (brown sugar, lots of vanilla extract, and chocolate chips) so when you eat it, it makes you think of the inside of a chocolate chip cookie.

1. Preheat the oven to 350°F.

2. Place the pie crust in 9-inch pie plate and crimp the edges as desired. Refrigerate until ready to fill.

3. Whisk together the butter, milk, eggs, brown sugar, granulated sugar, cornmeal, 2 tablespoons flour, salt, and vanilla.

4. Stir the chocolate chips into the filling mixture. Place prepared pie shell on a rimmed cookie sheet and pour the filling into the crust.

5. Bake for 35 to 40 minutes, until the crust is browned and the top of the pie is browned. It will still jiggle slightly in the middle. Cool completely before cutting.

6. Serve with whipped cream, ice cream, or chocolate sauce. Store loosely covered in the refrigerator for up to 3 days.

Tip As awesome as this pie is room temperature, it's amazing slightly warmed!

1 recipe All-Butter Pie Crust (page 64)

½ cup (1 stick) unsalted butter, melted

⅓ cup whole milk

4 large eggs

1 cup packed brown sugar

¼ cup granulated sugar

1 tablespoon cornmeal

2 tablespoons all-purpose flour

¼ teaspoon salt

1 tablespoon vanilla extract

½ cup milk or semisweet chocolate chips

Whipped cream, ice cream, or chocolate sauce, to serve

Cookies 'n' Cream Magic Bar Pie

Yield 10 servings **Prep Time** 25 minutes **Bake Time** 35 minutes

I have a major crush on magic bars. They really are magic you know. Just a few simple ingredients combined and baked together until firm create one of the most delicious desserts out there. Whether you call them magic bars or seven-layer bars, you won't be disappointed in this cookies 'n' cream version, especially because it comes in pie form!

25 chocolate sandwich cookies, crushed

¼ cup (½ stick) unsalted butter, melted

1 cup milk chocolate chips

1 cup sweetened shredded coconut

1 cup white chocolate chips

12 chocolate sandwich cookies, coarsely chopped

1 (14-ounce) can fat-free sweetened condensed milk

1. Preheat the oven to 350°F.

2. In a medium bowl, stir together the crushed sandwich cookies and melted butter with a fork. Press into the bottom and up the sides of a 9 or 9½-inch pie plate.

3. Sprinkle the milk chocolate chips, coconut, white chocolate chips, and additional chopped sandwich cookies over the crust. Pour the sweetened condensed milk over the filling. (Note: If your sweetened condensed milk is too thick to pour, transfer it to a microwave-safe bowl and heat on high for 15 to 20 seconds.)

4. Bake for 25 to 35 minutes, until the top seems set and not gooey. Cool completely before slicing. Store covered at room temperature for up to 4 days.

Tip This pie is not limited to cookies and cream! Think outside the box; the magic bar is one of the most versatile recipes out there. Add your favorite flavors with your favorite crust and you'll have a whole new pie!

Milky Way Brownie Pie

Yield 12 servings   **Prep Time** 15 minutes   **Bake Time** 45 minutes

I love taking candy and turning it into something completely different, because seeing what can happen is so much fun. That's what this pie is all about! The brownie batter is made with melted Milky Way candy bars, so it has the texture of a brownie but tastes like the candy. It's the perfect way to have your candy bar . . . and your brownie pie too.

1. Preheat the oven to 350°F. Place the pie crust in 9-inch pie plate, crimp the edges as desired, and refrigerate until the filling is ready.

2. Place 10 of the unwrapped Milky Way candy bars in a medium saucepan with the butter. Warm over medium-low heat, stirring constantly, until the candy bars melt. The mixture will be thick and goopy. Remove from the heat and stir in the sugar and cocoa powder. Stir in the eggs one at a time, then add vanilla and salt. Slowly stir in the flour. Pour into the prepared pie shell.

3. Place pie on a rimmed cookie sheet and bake for 35 to 45 minutes, until a toothpick comes out with a few crumbs on it. While the pie is baking, unwrap the remaining Milky Way candy bars. Slice each bar into 6 or 7 slices.

4. When the pie comes out of the oven, arrange the sliced candy bars in a sunburst pattern around the pie. Place back in the oven for 1 minute. Remove and cool completely before slicing.

5. Serve with ice cream or whipped cream, if desired. Best served and kept at room temperature. Store covered with plastic wrap or in an airtight container. Pie will last 4 days at room temperature.

1 recipe All-Butter Pie Crust (page 64)

22 to 24 Fun-Size Milky Way candy bars, divided

6 tablespoons (¾ stick) unsalted butter

¾ cup granulated sugar

1 tablespoon unsweetened cocoa powder

2 large eggs

1 teaspoon vanilla extract

¼ teaspoon salt

½ cup all-purpose flour

Ice cream or whipped cream, to serve

Tip You can skip the rings of Milky Way bars on top and just top with whipped cream or ice cream, if you wish.

Elvis Hand Pies

Yield 10 pies **Prep Time** 30 minutes **Bake Time** 18 minutes

I have a soft spot in my heart for Elvis. I'd never thought twice about him until my tenth wedding anniversary, when my husband surprised me with a vow renewal service at the Graceland Wedding Chapel in Las Vegas. The officiant? Elvis, of course! Ever since, I've been obsessed with the combination of peanut butter and banana. I'd never realized how good the flavor is. It goes great in everything, not just sandwiches. These hand pies are a combination of classic pie and the Elvis Sandwich, and they're perfect for thinking about the King—or just for a quick morning breakfast!

1 recipe All-Butter Pie Crust
(page 64)

6 teaspoons creamy or
crunchy peanut butter

½ banana, sliced

Honey, as needed

1 egg, lightly beaten

Granulated sugar, for sprinkling

Tip These pies are not limited to peanut butter and banana! Use your favorite jam, or replace the bananas with chocolate chips for a peanut buttery chocolate treat!

1. Roll out the pie crust dough to ¼ inch thick. Refrigerate for 30 minutes.

2. Preheat the oven to 375°F. Line a cookie sheet with parchment paper or a silicone baking mat.

3. Cut circles of crust using a 2½-inch round cookie cutter, rerolling the dough as needed. You will get about 20 circles.

4. Lay out 10 circles. Place a heaping ½ teaspoon peanut butter in the center of each and top with one slice of banana. Drizzle with a little honey.

5. Using your finger, wipe a little bit of the beaten egg around the edges of the crust. Top with a second circle of dough and press lightly. Press with the tines of a fork to seal. (The egg acts as glue so the pie stays together.) Repeat with remaining pies and then pierce the top of each a few times with a fork. Place on the prepared cookie sheet.

6. Again using your finger, rub a little egg over the top of each pie. Sprinkle with a pinch of sugar. Bake for 13 to 18 minutes, until the bottoms start to turn golden. The pies will still be somewhat pale in color. Cool on cookie sheet at least 5 minutes before eating. Store in an airtight container in the refrigerator. Best eaten within 2 days.

Turtle Pudding Pie

Yield 8 servings **Prep Time** 30 minutes **Bake Time** 15 minutes **Chill Time** 6 hours

My mom loves Turtles (the candy, not the animal, although we did have a turtle for a hot minute when I was a kid). I remember that when we'd get a box of them on Valentine's Day they'd last less than a day. This pie was inspired by Mom's favorite candy: a chocolate pecan crust, chocolate pudding filling, and caramel topping. It's a deconstructed Turtle—in a pie!

1½ cups pecans, divided

1½ cups chocolate wafer cookie crumbs (about 25 cookies)

6 tablespoons (¾ stick) unsalted butter, melted

⅔ cup granulated sugar

¼ teaspoon salt

¼ cup unsweetened cocoa powder

3 tablespoons cornstarch

2 cups whole milk

1 teaspoon vanilla extract

¼ cup semisweet or milk chocolate chips

20 unwrapped soft caramel candies

¼ cup heavy whipping cream

1. Preheat the oven to 350°F. Spread all the pecans on a cookie sheet and bake for 3 to 5 minutes, until toasted. Shake the pan a little after every minute and do not walk away from the oven. As soon as you smell them, they're done (and on their way to burning!). Let cool.

2. Finely chop ¾ cup of the toasted pecans. Stir together the cookie crumbs, finely chopped pecans, and melted butter. Press into the bottom and up the sides of a 9-inch pie plate. Bake for 10 minutes. Let cool before making the filling, about 1 hour.

3. Stir together the sugar, salt, cocoa powder, cornstarch, and milk in a medium saucepan. Cook over low heat until thickened, stirring constantly, 4 to 7 minutes. Remove from the heat and stir in the vanilla and chocolate chips until smooth. Pour into the prepared crust. Let cool for 30 minutes.

4. Place the caramels and heavy whipping cream in a microwave-safe bowl. Microwave on high for about 1½ to 2 minutes, in 30-second increments, stirring between each to help melt the caramel. Once the caramel is completely melted, place in the refrigerator to cool for 10 to 15 minutes (you want it cool, but not too thick to pour and spread). Coarsely chop remaining the ¾ cup pecans.

(continued on page 76)

5. Once the caramel has cooled, drizzle it very carefully over the pudding. You want it to be a separate layer, so don't pour it too fast or it will just mix into the pudding. Spread it to the edges of the pie. Sprinkle the pecans over the pie and refrigerate until set, at least 4 hours, before slicing. Store loosely covered and serve straight from the refrigerator; the caramel gets very drippy as it sits out. The pie will be good for up to 3 days.

Tip You can find the chocolate wafer cookies at most grocery stores, sometimes near the ice cream toppings. If you can't find them, you can use Oreos or a similar cookie instead.

Cake & Cupcake Creations

I love the Julia Child quote, "A party without cake is just a meeting." There has to be cake! As much as I love a plain vanilla cake, playing with the flavors and frostings of cakes and cupcakes to turn them into something fabulously different is incredibly gratifying. Whether it's a pie turned into a cupcake or a cake that's really a cookie, these recipes are perfect for your next meeting-turned-party.

Peanut Butter Cookie Cake

Yield 8 to 12 servings **Prep Time** 25 minutes **Bake Time** 25 minutes

Who doesn't love a huge peanut butter cookie? They're the number-one flavor in our house! If someone asks you for a cookie for their birthday, this is a great way to make them a cake— that's also a cookie! Covered with chocolate frosting and filled with colorful candies, this would be the perfect celebration cake!

Make the Cookie Cake

1. In the bowl of a stand mixer fitted with the paddle attachment, cream together the butter, peanut butter, brown sugar, and granulated sugar, about 1 minute. Add the egg, vanilla, milk, baking soda, and salt, and mix until combined. Slowly add the flour and mix until dough just comes together, scraping the sides of the bowl as necessary. Stir in the M&Ms or chocolate chips.

2. Spray a 9 or 10-inch round cake pan with cooking spray or line with foil and spray with cooking spray for easy removal and cleanup. Press the dough into the pan. Refrigerate for 30 minutes.

3. Preheat the oven to 350°F. When the dough is cold, bake for 20 to 25 minutes, until the top is golden brown. Let cool completely before frosting.

Make the Frosting

1. Using an electric hand mixer or stand mixer fitted with the paddle attachment, beat the butter until smooth. Slowly mix in the powdered sugar and cocoa powder. Mix in the salt, vanilla, and 2 teaspoons of the milk. Add the remaining 2 or 3 teaspoons of milk as needed to reach the desired consistency.

2. Place the frosting in a pastry bag fitted with a 1M tip and frost the outer ring of the cake. Dust with sprinkles, if using.

Tip Try substituting the M&Ms with any sort of candy or chocolate chip you love. Peanut butter cups make a fabulous cookie cake!

Cookie Cake

½ cup (1 stick) unsalted butter, softened

¾ cup creamy peanut butter

¾ cup packed brown sugar

¼ cup granulated sugar

1 large egg

1 teaspoon vanilla extract

1 tablespoon whole milk

½ teaspoon baking soda

½ teaspoon salt

1½ cups all-purpose flour

1 cup M&Ms or chocolate chips

Frosting

½ cup (1 stick) unsalted butter, softened

2 cups powdered sugar

½ cup unsweetened cocoa powder

Pinch of salt

2 teaspoons vanilla extract

4 to 5 teaspoons whole milk

Sprinkles, if desired

Carrot Cake Cheesecake Cupcakes

Yield 12 cupcakes **Prep Time** 45 minutes **Bake Time** 22 minutes **Cool Time** 3 hours

I love giving baked goods to say thank you to people. A few years ago, a friend of ours was doing some work around our house, and I wanted to make him something special as a thank you. I asked him what his two favorite desserts were and he told me carrot cake and cheesecake. That's how these cupcakes were born: half carrot cake and half cheesecake, topped with cream cheese frosting (like all carrot cakes should be). He enjoyed the thanks, and I hope you like them too!

Cake

1 large egg

¼ cup unsweetened applesauce

¼ cup vegetable oil

¼ cup packed brown sugar

¼ granulated sugar

½ teaspoon vanilla extract

½ teaspoon baking soda

½ teaspoon baking powder

¼ teaspoon salt

½ teaspoon ground cinnamon

½ cup all-purpose flour

½ cup shredded carrots (about 1 medium-large carrot)

½ cup chopped pecans (optional)

Make the Cake

1. Preheat the oven to 350°F. Line a standard 12-cup cupcake pan with paper liners.

2. In a large bowl, beat together the egg, applesauce, oil, brown sugar, granulated sugar, and vanilla using an electric hand mixer. Mix in the baking soda, baking powder, salt, and cinnamon. Gently stir in the flour, then stir in the carrots and pecans, if using. Pour 2 tablespoons of batter into each prepared muffin cup (use your 2-tablespoon cookie scoop if you have one). Not all carrots are created equal; some will have more wetness than others, creating more or less batter. You can make a few extra cupcakes if you have extra batter. Set aside.

(continued on page 82)

Cheesecake

8 ounces (1 package) cream cheese, at room temperature

2 tablespoons sour cream, at room temperature

¼ cup granulated sugar

1 large egg

1 teaspoon vanilla extract

Cream Cheese Frosting

½ cup (1 stick) unsalted butter, softened

8 ounces (1 package) cream cheese, softened

4 cups powdered sugar

1 teaspoon vanilla extract

1 teaspoon heavy whipping cream (optional, for consistency)

Tip This method is not limited to carrot cake alone! You can use your favorite cake flavor to make lots of different kinds of cheesecake cupcakes.

Make the Cheesecake

1. In the bowl of a stand mixer fitted with the paddle attachment, beat the cream cheese until smooth. Mix in the sour cream, sugar, egg, and vanilla. Beat until all or most of the lumps are gone. (Be sure that your ingredients are all at room temperature to avoid lumps.) Divide equally among the carrot cake batter in the muffin cups, being sure not to fill them more than ⅔ full.

2. Bake for 16 to 22 minutes, until the cheesecake is no longer runny and a toothpick inserted in the center of a cupcake comes out with only crumbs stuck to it. Cool pans on a wire rack to room temperature and then refrigerate for at least 2 hours before frosting.

Make the Cream Cheese Frosting

1. Using a hand mixer or a stand mixer fitted with the paddle attachment, cream together the butter and cream cheese until fluffy. Slowly add the powdered sugar, then mix in the vanilla. If your frosting is too stiff to pipe, add the heavy whipping cream. Mix until smooth.

2. Cover each cupcake with the frosting. For beautiful cupcakes, transfer the frosting to a piping bag fitted with a 1M tip for decorating. Any leftover frosting can be frozen for later use. Store the cupcakes loosely covered in the refrigerator for up to 4 days.

Death by Chocolate Brownie Cake

Yield 12 servings **Prep Time** 1 hour **Cook Time** 30 minutes **Chill Time** About 2 hours

This cake is the ultimate chocolate experience. Brownies get baked in round cake pans, layered with chocolate ganache filling, and frosted with a rich chocolate buttercream. Warning: Die-hard chocolate fans only! It's death by chocolate cake...in a brownie!

Make the Brownies

1. Preheat the oven to 350°F. Butter and flour two 9-inch round pans and line the bottoms with parchment paper. Then butter and flour the parchment. (You can also use the cooking spray with flour in it.)

2. Place the two baking chocolates and butter in a large, microwave-safe bowl. Microwave on high power for 2 to 3 minutes, stirring every 30 seconds, until the chocolate is smooth. Stir in the sugar. Add the eggs, vanilla, salt, and cocoa, and stir well. Add the flour and stir carefully.

3. Divide the batter between the pans and spread to the edges (batter will be thick). Bake for 21 to 25 minutes, until a toothpick inserted 2 inches from the edge of the pan comes out with just a touch of crumbs. Set pans on a wire rack to cool completely before removing brownies from pans.

(continued on next page)

Brownies

2 ounces unsweetened baking chocolate, coarsely chopped

3 ounces semisweet baking chocolate, coarsely chopped

1 cup (2 sticks) unsalted butter

2⅓ cups granulated sugar

4 large eggs

1 tablespoon vanilla extract

½ teaspoon salt

2 tablespoons unsweetened cocoa powder

1⅓ cups all-purpose flour

Filling

1½ cups walnuts, divided

1¾ cups semisweet mini chocolate chips, divided

½ cup heavy whipping cream

Frosting

1 cup (2 sticks) unsalted butter, softened

2 cups powdered sugar

½ cup unsweetened cocoa powder

¼ teaspoon salt

1 tablespoon vanilla extract

3 to 4 tablespoons heavy whipping cream, as needed

Tip Try using pecans or cashews instead of the walnuts, or you can leave them out altogether!

Make the Filling

1. Spread the walnuts on a cookie sheet and toast in the 350°F oven for 3 to 5 minutes, stirring every minute, until toasted. Do not walk away from the oven; they can burn quickly. Place in a bowl and set aside.

2. Bring 1 inch of water to a boil in a small pan. Place 1 cup of the mini chocolate chips and the heavy whipping cream in a bowl that will fit on top of the pan but not touch the water. Stir until the mixture is melted and smooth. Remove from the heat, let sit at room temperature for about 15 minutes, then refrigerate until thick enough to spread, 30 to 40 minutes.

Make the Frosting

1. With a hand mixer or a stand mixer fitted with the paddle attachment, beat the butter on low until smooth. Slowly beat in the powdered sugar until crumbly. Beat in the cocoa, salt, and vanilla. Add the heavy whipping cream, 1 tablespoon at a time, until you reach your desired consistency.

Assemble the Cake

1. Finely chop the toasted walnuts.

2. Place half the frosting in a pastry bag fitted with a large round tip or a 1M tip. Place the first brownie layer on a cake stand and pipe frosting around the edge, creating a barrier for the filling. Place the filling in the center and spread to the edges. Sprinkle with ⅓ cup of the chopped walnuts. Place the second brownie layer on top of the first. Frost the top and sides with the frosting. Place the remaining walnuts around the edges. Pipe a border around the top of the cake and fill the center with the remaining ¾ cup mini chocolate chips. Refrigerate for at least 30 minutes before serving. Store loosely covered at room temperature; the cake will stay fresh up to 5 days.

Strawberry Pie Cupcakes

Yield 12 cupcakes   **Prep Time** 30 minutes   **Cook Time** 30 minutes

When I was a kid, we'd have family gatherings every summer and always get a white sheet cake filled with fresh berries and topped with whipped cream frosting. These cupcakes are the pie version of that cake: a vanilla cupcake filled with strawberry pie filling, iced with a vanilla buttercream, and topped with a pie crust dipper.

Make the Strawberry Filling

1. Place 1 cup of the strawberries in a small saucepan with the sugar and ⅓ cup of the water. Cook, stirring occasionally, over medium-low heat for 10 minutes. In a small bowl, mix the remaining ¼ cup water with the cornstarch and then add it to the cooking strawberries. Cook until thick, about 1 minute, stirring constantly. It will thicken very quickly. Cool completely, either at room temperature or in the refrigerator. Stir in the remaining uncooked berries. Store in the refrigerator until the cupcakes are ready.

Make the Cupcakes

1. Preheat the oven to 350°F. Line a standard 12-cup cupcake pan with paper liners.

2. Whisk together the flour, baking powder, and salt in a medium bowl.

3. Place the melted butter in a large bowl and mix in the sugar with a hand mixer for 30 seconds until thick and yellow. Add the eggs one at a time, beating after each addition. Beat in the vanilla.

4. Add the flour mixture and buttermilk alternately, starting and ending with the flour. Don't overmix! Divide the batter among the paper liners, filling each one two-thirds full. Bake for 14 to 15 minutes, until a toothpick inserted into a cupcake comes out clean. Cool completely before frosting

Strawberry Filling

2 cups hulled and quartered strawberries (about 12 ounces), divided

½ cup granulated sugar

⅓ cup plus ¼ cup water, divided

2 tablespoons cornstarch

Cupcakes

1½ cups all-purpose flour

1 teaspoon baking powder

½ teaspoon salt

6 tablespoons (¾ stick) unsalted butter, melted

1 cup granulated sugar

3 large eggs

1 tablespoon vanilla extract

⅔ cup buttermilk

(continued on next page)

Frosting

½ cup (1 stick) unsalted butter, softened

Pinch of salt

2 cups powdered sugar

1 tablespoon vanilla extract

2 tablespoons heavy whipping cream

12 Pie Crust Dippers (page 108), for garnish (optional)

Make the Frosting

1. Using an electric hand mixer or stand mixer fitted with the paddle attachment, beat the butter until creamy. Beat in the salt and 1 cup of powdered sugar at a time until it's all added. Beat in the vanilla and heavy whipping cream. Transfer the frosting to a pastry bag fitted with a 1M tip.

Assemble the Cupcakes

1. Cut out the center of each cupcake, about 1½ inches in diameter and ½ to ¾ inch to deep. Fill the cupcake with just over a tablespoon of the strawberry filling. Pipe frosting around the edge of the cupcake to look like the whipped cream on a classic strawberry pie. Top with a pie crust dipper. Store loosely covered in refrigerator.

Tip These aren't limited to strawberry! Use your favorite berry instead, or use lemon curd for a lemon pie cupcake.

Snickers Cake Roll

Yield 12 servings **Prep Time** 30 minutes **Bake Time** 10 minutes **Chill Time** 4 to 12 hours

For a long time, I was scared of making a cake roll, but when I did it, I found that it's easier than it looks! The tricks are to roll it when it's still burn-your-hands hot and to use lots of powdered sugar so it doesn't stick to the towel. Filled with a peanut butter marshmallow fluff and caramel filling, this cake tastes just like a Snickers bar!

Make the Cake

1. Preheat the oven to 350°F. Line a 10 x 15-inch jelly roll pan with foil and spray with cooking spray (I like to use the spray with flour). This makes it easy to remove your cake from the pan while it is still hot.

2. In the bowl of a stand mixer fitted with the whisk attachment or in a large bowl with a hand mixer, beat the eggs at high speed for 5 minutes, until frothy and dark yellow. Beat in the sugar, cocoa, and vanilla.

3. In a medium bowl, whisk together salt, baking powder, and flour. Stir the dry ingredients into the wet just until blended.

4. Spread the batter in the prepared pan. It will be in a very thin layer and you will need to use a wooden spoon or spatula to spread it to all the corners of the pan. Bake for 8 to 10 minutes until it springs back when you touch it.

5. While the cake is baking, set a clean kitchen towel out on a large work surface. Sprinkle liberally with the powdered sugar. As soon as the cake comes out of the oven, being careful not to burn your fingers, turn it over on the kitchen towel sprinkled with powdered sugar. Remove the foil carefully.

6. Working from the short end, fold the edge of the towel over the cake. Roll tightly, rolling the cake up into the towel. Let cool completely while rolled, at least 1 hour.

Cake

3 large eggs

¾ cup granulated sugar

¼ cup unsweetened cocoa powder

1 teaspoon vanilla extract

¼ teaspoon salt

1 teaspoon baking powder

¾ cup all-purpose flour

¼ cup powdered sugar, for rolling

(continued on next page)

Filling

⅓ cup creamy peanut butter

1 (7-ounce) jar marshmallow crème

15 unwrapped soft caramel candies

2 tablespoons whole milk

½ cup peanuts, finely chopped

Topping

½ cup semisweet or milk chocolate chips

½ cup heavy whipping cream

½ cup peanuts, coarsely chopped

Tip Don't fret if your cake roll cracks a little. The chocolate topping and the peanuts can hide all sorts of blemishes. For a picture tutorial on how to roll a cake, check out my blog at crazyforcrust.com.

Make the Filling

1. Once cake is cooled, make the filling. Place the peanut butter in a microwave-safe bowl and microwave on high for 30 seconds. Add the marshmallow fluff and heat for 10 more seconds. Stir until mixed. Unroll the cake carefully and spread a thin layer of the marshmallow mixture over it. The mixture is pretty sticky, so be sure not to use too much side-to-side motion when frosting or it will pull up crumbs from the cake.

2. Heat the caramels and milk in a second microwave-safe bowl on high for about 1 minute, stirring after 30 seconds. After 1 minute, stir until all the caramels are melted. If they still aren't melted, heat in additional 15-second increments, stirring between each. Once the caramel is melted, let it cool for 1 minute, then stir in the chopped peanuts. Spread a thin layer over the marshmallow layer.

3. Carefully roll the cake again. Try not to press it too much or it may crack. Roll it back up and wrap it in plastic wrap, then refrigerate for at least 2 hours or overnight.

Make the Topping

1. Place the chocolate chips and heavy whipping cream in a microwave-safe bowl or glass measuring cup. Microwave for about 45 seconds on high, then whisk until smooth and all the chocolate is melted, heating for an additional 15 seconds if necessary. Let the chocolate refrigerate for about 1 hour. If the chocolate gets too hard, you can microwave it on high in 5 to 10-second increments, until it reaches a pourable consistency.

2. When ready to assemble the cake, unwrap it and place it on a rack over a cookie sheet. Pour the chocolate evenly over the cake. The excess chocolate will end up on the cookie sheet. Sprinkle the top with chopped peanuts. Refrigerate for 30 minutes to 1 hour before cutting. Store loosely covered in the refrigerator, but this cake is best served at room temperature. Cake will keep for up to 4 days.

S'morescake

Yield 10 servings Prep Time 50 minutes Bake Time 30 minutes

There's something about the s'more that makes it so fun (and easy) to turn into different desserts. This cake may look grand, but it's really easy to make. A graham cracker crust is topped with a flourless chocolate cake that's so rich and dense, and it's perfect paired with the light and fluffy meringue topping. Don't be afraid of meringue; it's easier than it looks, believe me. And, if you have a kitchen torch, it's so much fun to brown!

Crust

1½ cups graham cracker crumbs

2 tablespoons granulated sugar

6 tablespoons (¾ stick) unsalted butter, melted

Filling

½ cup (1 stick) unsalted butter

6 ounces semisweet chocolate, broken into pieces

¾ cup granulated sugar

4 large eggs

¼ teaspoon salt

1 teaspoon vanilla extract

1 teaspoon brewed coffee (optional)

Make the Crust

1. Preheat the oven to 350°F. Spray a 9 or 10-inch springform pan with cooking spray.

2. In a medium bowl, stir together the graham cracker crumbs, sugar, and melted butter with a fork. Press into the bottom of the prepared pan. Freeze while preparing the filling.

Make the Filling

1. Combine the butter and semisweet chocolate in a large microwave-safe bowl and microwave on high in 30-second increments, stirring between each, until melted and smooth, about 1½ to 2 minutes total.

2. Whisk in the sugar, eggs, salt, vanilla, and coffee, if using. (The coffee will enhance the flavor of the chocolate.)

3. Pour the filling into the prepared crust. Bake for 25 to 30 minutes. The cake will be just a little bit jiggly in the center. Cool completely in the pan before frosting with meringue. You can make the cake ahead and refrigerate it, covered, overnight before frosting.

(continued on page 94)

Meringue

5 large egg whites (about 5¼ ounces)

¾ cup plus 3 teaspoons granulated sugar (about 5¼ ounces)

1 teaspoon vanilla extract

Make the Meringue

1. Place the egg whites and sugar in a large heat-safe bowl. Place the bowl over a saucepan filled with 1 to 2 inches of boiling water (do not let the bowl touch the water). Whisk and cook over medium heat until the egg whites reach about 160°F, 10 to 12 minutes (you can use a candy thermometer to measure the temperature). Pour the egg whites into the bowl of a stand mixer fitted with a whisk attachment, add the vanilla, and beat on medium speed until stiff peaks form, about 5 minutes. (You can use a hand mixer for this step, but it will take quite a bit longer.)

2. Place the meringue in a pastry bag with a large round tip or a 1M tip and pipe onto the cooled cake. For the toasted look, use a kitchen torch, or you can place the cake on a cookie sheet and put it under the broiler for 1 to 2 minutes at most. (If using the broiler, do not walk away from the stove! Watch the cake the entire time to make sure it doesn't burn.)

3. Store covered in the refrigerator, but this cake is best served the same day as the meringue is made. After about a day, the meringue starts to weep. You can make the cake up to 2 days ahead of time and add the meringue right before serving.

Tip If you don't have a pastry bag handy, just use a gallon-size resealable plastic bag with one tip cut off.

New Takes on Cheesecake

Cheesecake is one of those things I cannot have in my house. I will attack it with a fork, then look up guiltily when my husband catches me in the dark with the springform pan on my lap. Full cheesecakes can be gorgeous showstoppers for parties, but cheesecake bars and cookies are more manageable for everyday life because they're easier to freeze and give away. This chapter has plenty of choices for you, from bars to ice cream, from easy to stunning. I hope you enjoy your fork-in-the-dark moments with these recipes like I did while I was creating them.

A quick tip for always-successful cheesecakes: Make sure all your ingredients are at room temperature. This helps avoid a lumpy cheesecake!

Cheesecake Swirl Brownie Bars

Yield 24 bars **Prep Time** 20 minute **Cook Time** 30 minutes **Chill Time** 4 hours

I love cheesecake swirled brownie bars, but usually they're missing a crust. These are the perfect combination of brownie and cheesecake, complete with a graham cracker crust!

Crust

1½ cups graham cracker crumbs (about 8 whole graham crackers)

½ cup (1 stick) unsalted butter, melted

1 tablespoon granulated sugar

Brownies

2 ounces unsweetened baking chocolate, coarsely chopped

2 ounces semisweet baking chocolate, coarsely chopped

¾ cup (1½ sticks) unsalted butter

1¾ cups granulated sugar

2 tablespoons unsweetened cocoa powder

3 large eggs

1 tablespoon vanilla extract

¼ teaspoon salt

1 cup all-purpose flour

Cheesecake

8 ounces (1 package) cream cheese, at room temperature

¼ cup sour cream, room temperature

1 large egg

¼ cup granulated sugar

½ teaspoon vanilla extract

Make the Crust

1. Preheat the oven to 350°F. Spray a 9 x 13-inch pan with cooking spray or line with foil and spray with cooking spray for easy cleanup.

2. In a medium bowl, stir together the graham cracker crumbs, butter, and sugar with a fork. Press into the bottom of the prepared pan. Bake for 5 minutes. While the crust is baking, make the brownies.

Make the Brownies

1. Melt both baking chocolates and the butter together in a large microwave-safe bowl. Microwave on high in 30-second increments, stirring between each, until the mixture is smooth. Stir in the sugar. Stir in the cocoa, eggs and vanilla. Carefully stir in the salt and flour. Pour over the hot crust in the pan.

Make the Cheesecake

1. Mix the cream cheese with a hand mixer until smooth. Mix in sour cream. Beat in the egg, sugar, and vanilla. Place spoonfuls of the cheesecake mixture on top of the brownies, then swirl with the back of a wooden spoon.

2. Bake for 28 to 35 minutes, or until the top is no longer glossy and a toothpick inserted 2 inches from the edge of the pan comes out with just a trace of chocolate. Cool completely to room temperature, then refrigerate for at least 2 hours before cutting into bars. Store in an airtight container in the refrigerator for up to 4 days.

Tip Try these with a chocolate cookie crust. You'll be amazed!

Cookies 'n' Cream Cheesecake Ice Cream

Yield 1 quart **Prep Time** 5 minutes plus churning time **Chill Time** 12 hours

I often joke with my husband that I could compete on one of those food-eating shows, the kind where the contestant is challenged to eat a ton in a short period of time. I could totally win any of those competitions—if it's dessert. Oreo cookies are one challenge I could do, no problem. Ice cream and cheesecake are two others I'd win, hands down. Marry the three together and you have something I'll eat until I collapse!

1. Place the cream cheese in a large microwave-safe bowl. Heat on high for 30 to 45 seconds until you can stir it with a wooden spoon. Stir in the sugar, then whisk in the heavy whipping cream, milk, vanilla, salt, and lemon juice. Whisk until smooth. Cover and refrigerate for 4 hours.

2. Place the sandwich cookies in a gallon-size resealable plastic bag. Whack the bag with a rolling pin until the cookies are crushed (careful—some holes will be made in the bag during the crushing). Set aside.

3. Once completely chilled, add the ice cream mixture to your ice cream machine and churn according to the manufacturer's instructions. During the last 5 minutes of churning, add the crushed cookies. Once it's finished, transfer to a resealable container and freeze for at least 8 hours before eating. Store in the freezer.

Tip You're not limited to Oreos for this ice cream! Use your favorite flavor cookie, candy, or even pie filling for a variation on the cheesecake flavor.

4 ounces (½ package) cream cheese, at room temperature

1½ cups granulated sugar

1 cup heavy whipping cream

1½ cups whole milk

1 teaspoon vanilla extract

Pinch of salt

1 teaspoon fresh lemon juice

15 chocolate sandwich cookies

Oatmeal Cookie Cheesecake Bars

Yield 24 bars **Prep Time** 30 minutes **Bake Time** 30 minutes

Oatmeal cookies and cheesecake make a fabulous pairing. Top with some toffee bits when they come out of the oven, and the flavor becomes like a crème brûlée!

Cookie

½ cup (1 stick) unsalted butter, softened

⅔ cup packed brown sugar

½ cup granulated sugar

1 large egg

1 teaspoon vanilla extract

½ teaspoon baking soda

¼ teaspoon salt

1 teaspoon ground cinnamon

1 cup all-purpose flour

1½ cups quick-cooking oats

Cheesecake

8 ounces (½ package) cream cheese, at room temperature

⅓ cup sour cream, at room temperature

⅓ cup granulated sugar

1 teaspoon vanilla extract

1 large egg

1 cup toffee bits

Make the Cookie

1. Preheat the oven to 350°F. Spray a 9 x 13-inch pan with cooking spray or line with foil and spray with cooking spray for easy cleanup.

2. In the bowl of a stand mixer fitted with the paddle attachment, cream together the butter, brown sugar, and granulated sugar on low speed. Beat in the egg and vanilla. Mix in the baking soda, salt, and cinnamon. Slowly beat in the flour. Mix in the oats.

3. Press the dough into the prepared pan in a thin layer. The dough will be sticky, so spray your hands with cooking spray first.

Make the Cheesecake

1. Wash and dry the mixer bowl and paddle attachment. Beat the cream cheese and sour cream together until smooth. Mix in the sugar, vanilla, and egg and beat until smooth; try to get all the lumps out, but some may remain. Pour and spread over the cookie layer.

2. Bake for 25 to 30 minutes, until the top bounces back to a light touch. Immediately after removing from the oven, sprinkle the toffee bits evenly across the top of the bars. Let cool completely in pan before cutting into bars. Store in the refrigerator in a sealed container. Do not freeze (the toffee chips will dissolve).

Tip Omit the toffee bits and add 1 cup of butterscotch, white, or chocolate chips to the cookie dough batter before pressing in to the pan.

Chocolate Cheesecake Sandwich Cookies

Yield 28 cookies, 14 sandwiches **Prep Time** 25 minutes **Chill Time** 1 hour **Bake Time** 12 minutes

Sometimes you want cheesecake flavor but you really don't want to make a whole cheesecake. These cookies are perfect for those days. The soft chocolate cookie is filled with a no-bake cheesecake. The rich flavor comes from using a dark chocolate cocoa powder, which adds a layer of flavor you didn't even know you were missing!

1. Place semisweet chocolate in a small, microwave safe bowl. Melt on high power in increments of 30 seconds, stirring between each, until melted and smooth. Let cool slightly.

2. In the bowl of a stand mixer fitted with the paddle attachment, beat together the butter, brown sugar, ½ cup of the granulated sugar, 1 teaspoon of the vanilla, and the eggs until smooth. Beat in the melted baking chocolate and cocoa powder. Beat in the salt, flour, and baking soda until well blended. Refrigerate the dough for 1 hour.

3. Preheat the oven to 350°F. Line 2 cookie sheets with parchment paper or silicone baking mats. Drop 2-tablespoon balls of cookie dough onto the cookie sheet about 2 inches apart.

4. Bake for 9 to 12 minutes, until the edges lose their sheen. Cool cookies 5 minutes on cookie sheets, then transfer to a rack to cool completely before continuing.

5. Mix the cream cheese in a large bowl with a hand mixer until smooth. Beat in the remaining 1½ teaspoons vanilla and ½ cup granulated sugar. Mix until smooth. Turn half of the cooled cookies upside down and place about 2 tablespoons of cheesecake mixture on each one. Top with a second cookie to form a sandwich. Store in an airtight container in the refrigerator for up to 1 week.

Tip Measure the dough with a 1-tablespoon cookie scoop for a smaller, more bite-size cookie sandwich!

2 ounces semisweet chocolate

¾ cup (1½ sticks) unsalted butter, softened

1 cup packed brown sugar

1 cup granulated sugar, divided

2½ teaspoons vanilla extract, divided

2 large eggs

2 tablespoons unsweetened Hershey's Special Dark cocoa powder

½ teaspoon salt

2¼ cups all-purpose flour

1 teaspoon baking soda

12 ounces (1½ packages) cream cheese, at room temperature

Lemon Bar Cheesecake

Yield 12 servings   Prep Time 45 minutes   Cook Time 1 hour 40 minutes   Chill Time 12 hours

I always told myself I hated lemon desserts, but then one day I tasted a lemon pie. It was love at first bite, and now I can't get enough! This Lemon Bar Cheesecake is one of my favorite lemon recipes ever. A lemon cheesecake on a thick shortbread crust is topped with a cooked lemon bar filling for some amazing sweet and tart flavor.

Lemon Bar Filling

6 tablespoons fresh lemon juice

1½ cups granulated sugar

3 tablespoons all-purpose flour

3 large eggs

Crust

½ cup (1 stick) unsalted butter, softened

¼ cup granulated sugar

1½ cups all-purpose flour

¼ teaspoon salt

Grated zest of 1 small lemon (about 1 teaspoon)

1 tablespoon cold water

Tip The cooked lemon bar mixture is a cross between a pudding and a curd. You can also spread it on toast or eat it with a spoon (which is what I really wanted to do!).

Make the Lemon Bar Filling

1. Whisk together the lemon juice, sugar, flour, and eggs in a medium saucepan. Warm over medium-low heat, stirring constantly, until the mixture thickens, 4 to 5 minutes. Remove from the heat and transfer to a bowl to cool. Cool to room temperature and then cover and refrigerate for at least 2 hours (or overnight).

Make the Crust

1. Preheat the oven to 350°F.

2. Mix the butter, sugar, flour, salt, lemon zest, and water with an electric mixer until the mixture starts to come together but is still in large crumbles (the texture of dough). If you're using a stand mixer, this process will take 1 to 2 minutes. It will take longer with a hand mixer. Press into the bottom and ½ inch up the sides of a 9½-inch springform pan that has been sprayed lightly with cooking spray. Bake for 14 to 18 minutes, until it starts to turn slightly golden brown.

3. Cool the crust for about 10 minutes, then wrap the bottom of the pan in two layers of heavy-duty aluminum foil. You will be baking the cheesecake in a water bath, and you want to make sure no water gets into the pan from the seam at the bottom. Bring a kettle of water to boil for the water bath.

(continued on page 106)

Cheesecake

16 ounces (2 packages) cream cheese, at room temperature

¾ cup granulated sugar

1 cup sour cream, at room temperature

3 large eggs, at room temperature

2 tablespoons all-purpose flour

2 tablespoons lemon juice

Grated zest of 1 small lemon (about 1 teaspoon)

½ teaspoon vanilla extract

Powdered sugar, raspberries, or lemon zest, for garnish

Make the Cheesecake

1. Make sure all the cheesecake ingredients are room temperature. The trick to avoiding lumps in a cheesecake is to start with everything the same temperature!

2. In a stand mixer fitted with the paddle attachment, beat the cream cheese until smooth. Beat in the sugar and sour cream until smooth. Beat in the eggs one at a time, until fully incorporated. Mix in the flour, lemon juice, lemon zest, and vanilla. Be sure to scrape down the sides and bottom of the bowl during mixing to get any clumps of cream cheese stuck to the sides or bottom. Pour the cheesecake into the crust.

3. Place half of the cold lemon bar mixture in a zip-top plastic bag and cut off one tip. Drizzle it evenly over the top of the cheesecake, then swirl it carefully with the back of a butter knife or wooden spoon.

4. Place the cheesecake in a large roasting pan. Place the pan in the center of the preheated oven. Pour the boiling water carefully in one corner of the pan, until it reaches about one-third to halfway up the cheesecake.

5. Bake for 60 to 70 minutes, until the cheesecake is just slightly jiggly in the center. Turn off the oven and let it sit for 1 hour. Remove from the oven and let cool completely, then cover and refrigerate overnight.

6. When ready to serve, carefully remove the ring of the springform pan and spread the remaining lemon bar mixture over the top of the cheesecake. Serve with a dusting of powdered sugar, raspberries, or lemon zest. Store loosely covered in the refrigerator for up to 4 days.

Double Dips

Before I started blogging, I had no idea that an appetizer could be sweet. Then one day a friend of mine made Cake Batter Dip and my whole world changed. A sweet dip to serve at a party as a dessert appetizer? That one idea opened up a whole new category of desserts: dips inspired by my other favorite treats. Try one of these at your next party—your friends will be amazed, I promise!

Pie Crust Dippers

Yield 18–22 dippers   Prep Time 20 minutes   Chill Time 30 minutes   Bake Time 14 minutes

For a really successful dessert dip, you need good dippers to go with it. One day I was making a cake batter dip for my blog, so I reached for a package of pie crusts and one of my favorite dippers was born! These are so easy to make and go with pretty much every sweet dip you could ever serve. Plus, it gives you an excuse to eat pie crust!

1 recipe All-Butter Pie Crust (page 64)

Granulated sugar, for topping

1. Line a cookie sheet with parchment paper or silicone baking mat. Roll out the pie crust dough to about $1/8$ inch thick. Use a 2-inch round cookie cutter to cut circles of crust, rerolling the dough as needed. Place the circles on the prepared cookie sheets. Refrigerate for 30 minutes. Before baking, sprinkle each dipper with a pinch of sugar.

2. Preheat the oven to 400°F. Bake for 12 to 14 minutes, until the bottoms are golden brown. Cool completely on cookie sheets before serving. Store in an airtight container at room temperature for up to 5 days.

Tip Use any small, shaped cookie cutter (no bigger than 2 inches) to make dippers that will fit any occasion!

Oreo Peanut Butter

Yield 8 ounces **Prep Time** 10 minutes

Have you ever made your own peanut butter? It's just so much better than store-bought, and it's one of the easiest things to make at home. One day, on a whim, I added some Oreos to my peanut butter and, oh my goodness, I couldn't believe the flavor. Beware: This peanut butter is very addicting. Hide your spoons!

1. Place the peanuts and sandwich cookies in a food processor and run continuously until a butter forms. Time will vary depending on your food processor's age and speed. Mine takes about 4 minutes to reach a creamy, buttery consistency. If your processor is older, or starts to feel hot during processing, stop the machine and let it rest a few minutes before continuing. The dip will go from crumbly to a ball and then smooth out, then become soft and smooth, like a natural peanut butter. That's when it's done.

2. Serve on toast, as a dip, or with a spoon. Store in an airtight container in the refrigerator for up to 2 weeks.

1½ cups honey roasted peanuts

10 chocolate sandwich cookies

Tip You're not limited to Oreos here—try your favorite cookie flavor! If you're not a peanut person, most other nuts also lend themselves to this method (but you may need to add a tablespoon or so of oil during processing to smooth it out).

Tiramisu Dip

Yield About 3 cups **Prep Time** 15 minutes

One Christmas, my husband and I stayed overnight in San Francisco and ate at this teeny little Italian restaurant. It was run by a couple from Florence, and the food was so good. I especially remember the tiramisu. I normally don't order dessert in restaurants, but I couldn't help myself, and I'm so glad I indulged. Our meal that night inspired this dip!

1½ teaspoons instant coffee or instant espresso

¼ cup hot water

1 cup cold heavy whipping cream

¾ cup plus 1 tablespoon powdered sugar, divided

8 ounces mascarpone cheese, at room temperature

1 teaspoon vanilla extract

1 ounce semisweet chocolate

Assorted Dippers: pound cake squares, angel food cake squares, shortbread cookies, or fruit

1. Add the instant coffee to the hot water and stir. Let cool.

2. Place the cold heavy whipping cream and 1 tablespoon of the powdered sugar in a large bowl or a stand mixer fitted with the whisk attachment. Beat until it becomes whipped cream and stiff peaks form.

3. Place the mascarpone in a large bowl with the remaining ¾ cup powdered sugar. Beat with a hand mixer until smooth. Mix in the vanilla and 2 tablespoons of the cooled coffee. Add more coffee to taste.

4. Grate about half of the chocolate into the mixture with a box grater or a Microplane grater. Stir. Fold in the whipped cream.

5. Place the dip in a serving bowl and grate the rest of the chocolate on top for garnish. Serve with dippers. Store covered with plastic wrap in the refrigerator for up to 3 days.

Tip Soft ladyfingers would be a good dipper for this recipe, but they're hard to find. Check with your grocer's bakery to see if they carry them; if not, pound cake or angel food cake (or any vanilla cupcake) would make a good substitute. You can also substitute cream cheese for the mascarpone if you cannot find it.

Peanut Butter Cookie Fondue

Yield 2 cups **Cook Time** 4 to 8 minutes

My favorite way to eat a cookie is warm, straight from the oven, when it's gooey and not quite set. That's what this fondue reminds me of. If you melted a peanut butter cookie you would end up with the flavor of this hot dip. It's the perfect sweet finish to a fondue dinner, and any time I can have my cookies dipped in more cookies, I'm a happy girl.

1. If you're using an electric fondue pot or mini Crock-Pot, preheat it.

2. Place the white chocolate chips, peanut butter, and heavy whipping cream in a medium saucepan. Warm over medium-low heat, stirring almost constantly, until melted and smooth. Pour into the fondue pot. Serve with assorted dippers. This is best served the day it's made.

Tip This dip makes about 1 pint of dip, which is perfect for my mini slow cooker. If you're using a larger fondue pot, you can double the recipe.

1½ cups white chocolate chips

¾ cup creamy peanut butter

¾ cup heavy whipping cream

Assorted Dippers: Cookies, marshmallows, fruit, pound cake, or Pie Crust Dippers (page 108)

Almond Joy Dip

Yield About 3 cups **Prep Time** 10 minutes

Growing up, my dad was the only one in our house who liked coconut. He'd take all the coconut candies from my Halloween basket, and occasionally I'd see him eating a Mounds bar. As an adult, I discovered how wrong I was about coconut: It's probably one of the most fabulous flavors ever! This dip is reminiscent of an Almond Joy candy bar: a sweet coconut base topped with almonds and chocolate fudge.

¾ cup fat-free sweetened condensed milk

2 cups shredded sweetened coconut

1 teaspoon vanilla extract

½ teaspoon imitation coconut extract (optional)

1 teaspoon whole milk

½ cup chopped almonds

1 tablespoon chocolate sauce or warmed hot fudge ice-cream topping

Assorted Dippers: chocolate cookies, graham crackers, or other cookies

1. In a large bowl, stir together the sweetened condensed milk and the coconut. Stir in the vanilla, coconut extract, if using, and milk. Reserve 1 teaspoon of the chopped almonds and stir in the rest. Place in serving bowl.

2. Place the warmed hot fudge topping or chocolate sauce in a zip-top plastic bag with one tip cut off. Drizzle over the dip, then sprinkle the reserved almonds on top. (If you prefer a more chocolatey dip, you can stir 2 tablespoons of the fudge topping into the mixture before placing it in the bowl.)

3. Serve with assorted dippers. Store covered with plastic wrap in the refrigerator for up to 4 days.

Tip Leave off the almonds and use a dark chocolate sauce, and you have a Mounds dip instead of Almond Joy!

Banana Cream Pie Dip

Yield About 3 cups **Prep Time** 20 minutes **Cook Time** 5 minutes **Chill Time** 4 hours

One of the first times my husband had dinner at my parents' house, they made a banana cream pie. I'd told them he loved bananas, which was true, but he didn't love banana desserts (or pudding for that matter). He didn't want to say anything, so he ate two entire slices! Years later, I still think about the look on his face when my mom served him the second piece. Every time I make a banana cream pie, I think of that night, because I love it even if he doesn't. This dip is inspired by a pie, but without the mess of serving it. Present it with some pie crust dippers and you have a great party dip that will feed a crowd!

1. Whisk together the granulated sugar, cornstarch, and salt in a medium saucepan. Whisk in the milk and place over medium heat. Whisk until there are no more lumps, then switch to a wooden spoon and cook, stirring constantly, until the mixture thickens, 4 to 5 minutes. Remove from the heat and stir in the vanilla. Transfer to a bowl and let cool to room temperature, then cover with plastic wrap and refrigerate for at least 4 hours or overnight.

2. Make the whipped cream: Beat the heavy whipping cream and powdered sugar in a stand mixer fitted with the whisk attachment (or use a hand mixer) until stiff peaks form.

3. Place the cold pudding in a large bowl. Dice 1 banana into very small pieces and stir into the pudding. Fold 1 cup of the whipped cream into the banana pudding.

(continued on next page)

⅔ cup granulated sugar

3 tablespoons cornstarch

¼ teaspoon salt

2 cups whole milk

1 tablespoon vanilla extract

1 cup cold heavy whipping cream

1 tablespoon powdered sugar

2 bananas, divided

Assorted items for dipping: Pie Crust Dippers (page 108), vanilla wafers, and/or graham crackers

4. To serve, slice the remaining banana into thin slices. Place banana slices around the sides of a 9-inch glass pie plate. Scoop the pudding into the pie plate and then pipe the remaining whipped cream around the edges. Refrigerate until ready to serve. Serve with assorted dippers.

5. This dip is best served the day it is assembled. Store leftovers covered with plastic wrap in refrigerator, but know that the bananas may turn color overnight. Dip will last up to 3 days in refrigerator.

Holiday Mash-Ups

My favorite thing about any holiday is the food. I'm a total sucker for serving cute or themed desserts at any party (or on a random Tuesday). While Christmas is the obvious dessert holiday, I think every occasion throughout the year has the potential for adorable sweetness!

Chocolate-Covered Strawberry Truffles

Yield 24 strawberries   **Prep Time** 45 minutes   **Chill Time** 2 to 4 hours

If there are two things you see a lot of on Valentine's Day, it's truffles and chocolate-covered strawberries. This recipe combines the two into one chocolatey treat that's perfect for your sweetheart. Chocolate truffles are stuffed inside a strawberry and then the whole thing is dipped in chocolate and sprinkles. If you ask me, the sprinkles are the best part (but I may be addicted to sprinkles so I might not be the best judge of that!).

10 ounces semisweet chocolate, divided

¼ cup heavy whipping cream

½ teaspoon vanilla extract

24 strawberries, washed and dried very well

Sprinkles

1. Chop 4 ounces of the chocolate and place it in a medium heat-safe bowl. Heat the heavy whipping cream in a small saucepan over low heat until just before it starts to boil. You can also heat it in the microwave on high for about 40 seconds. Pour over the chocolate. Let sit for 30 seconds or so, then whisk until smooth. If the chocolate doesn't want to melt all the way, you can heat it in the microwave on high in additional 10-second increments, whisking after each, until the mixture is smooth. Whisk in the vanilla. Cover and refrigerate until firm, 1 to 2 hours.

2. Line a cookie sheet with waxed paper. Once the chocolate is firm, scoop 1-tablespoon-sized balls and place on the prepared cookie sheet. Refrigerate for at least 30 minutes. You can also do this step the night before and refrigerate overnight; just wrap the cookie sheet in plastic wrap or place the truffles in a resealable container.

3. When you're ready to assemble the truffles, remove them from the refrigerator. Cut each ball in half, then roll to make them round. Refrigerate while preparing the strawberries.

4. Remove the green tops of the strawberries. Using a small knife, cut out about a dime-sized circle in the top of each strawberry. Gently press a truffle into each strawberry.

(continued on page 124)

5. Melt the remaining 6 ounces of chocolate. You can do this by placing them in a heat-safe bowl over a pot filled with 1 inch of boiling water, or you can heat it in the microwave on 50 percent power in 30-second increments, stirring after each. Place the sprinkles in a bowl. Line a cookie sheet with waxed paper. Dip the truffle side of each strawberry in the chocolate, dip in the sprinkles, and place it on the prepared cookie sheet. Refrigerate to set. Store, covered, in the refrigerator. These are best eaten the day they're made but will last up to 2 days when kept in the refrigerator.

Tip Try dipping the stuffed strawberries in white chocolate instead of semisweet for a tuxedo truffle!

Rainbow Sugar Cookie Pizza

Yield 12 servings   **Prep Time** 30 minutes   **Bake Time** 11 minutes

I'm kind of addicted to making food into rainbows. I just think there is something so pretty and mystical about them. When I was a little girl, my best friend and I would plan our "Rainbow Wedding" where all the bridesmaids would wear rainbow colors. My love of rainbows inspired the design on this sugar cookie pizza: The pizza is frosted with a layer of jam "sauce" and vanilla frosting "cheese," and the toppings are a rainbow of fruit. It's perfect for any St. Patrick's Day celebration or an adult rainbow-themed birthday party—which I fully intend on having!

Make the Cookie

1. Preheat the oven to 350°F. Spray a 12-inch round pizza pan with cooking spray.

2. Cream together the butter and sugar in the bowl of a stand mixer fitted with the paddle attachment. Beat in the egg, vanilla, and almond extract, if using. Beat in the baking soda, cream of tartar, and salt, then add the flour. Mix, scraping the sides of the bowl as needed, until the dough comes together.

3. Press the dough into the prepared pan. It helps to spray your hands with cooking spray so it doesn't stick to them. Bake for about 11 minutes, until it's just starting to turn golden on top. It may still be a little glossy on the top, but you don't want to overbake it. Cool completely in the pan before frosting.

(continued on page 127)

Cookie

¾ cup (1½ sticks) unsalted butter, softened

¾ cup granulated sugar

1 large egg

1 tablespoon vanilla extract

½ teaspoon almond extract (optional)

½ teaspoon baking soda

½ teaspoon cream of tartar

½ teaspoon salt

2 cups all-purpose flour

Make the Frosting

1. Beat the butter with a hand mixer in a large bowl. Add a pinch of salt and the powdered sugar, 1 cup at a time, mixing between each. Once it's crumbly, add the vanilla and 1 tablespoon of the milk. Mix until smooth. Add up to 1 more tablespoon of milk as needed to get a spreading consistency.

Topping

1. Spread jam on the cookie to for the "sauce," leaving a border around the edge like a traditional pizza. Spread the frosting over the jam carefully so it does not mix. Use an offset spatula, if you have one.

2. Arrange the fruit in a rainbow pattern on the cookie. Add the mini marshmallows for clouds. Depending on the kind of fruit you use, you should serve the cookie pizza immediately. This won't be as pretty the second day. The cookie can be baked and frosted up to one day ahead, but add the fruit right before serving. Store leftovers in an airtight container in the refrigerator.

Frosting

¼ cup (½ stick) unsalted butter, at room temperature

Pinch of salt

2 cups powdered sugar

1 teaspoon vanilla extract

1 to 2 tablespoons nonfat milk

Topping

3 tablespoons of your favorite flavor jam, at room temperature so it spreads

Rainbow-colored fruit (raspberries or strawberries, oranges or melon, pineapple or banana, green grapes or kiwi, and blueberries or red grapes)

Mini marshmallows

Peanut Butter Cheesecake Football Dip

Yield 4 cups **Prep Time** 25 minutes

My husband is a football fanatic. He plays in a fantasy league, and he's so committed to it that he usually travels to his draft each August. Since he's also addicted to peanut butter, I made this dip one year for the Super Bowl and it became an instant favorite. It's super simple to make, and it's full of peanut butter–cheesecake flavor. There isn't much in the world that is better than this dip!

¼ cup (1 stick) unsalted butter, softened

4 ounces (½ package) cream cheese, softened

1 cup creamy or crunchy peanut butter

½ teaspoon vanilla extract

¼ teaspoon salt

1½ to 2 cups powdered sugar, as needed

½ cup semisweet mini chocolate chips

Chocolate sprinkles or chocolate chips, for the outside of the football

Melted white chocolate or frosting, for the football laces

Pretzels, animal crackers, or cookies, to serve

1. With a hand mixer, cream together the butter, cream cheese, and peanut butter until mixed. Mix in the vanilla.

2. Add the powdered sugar, ½ cup at a time, and mix until combined. (If you want a stiffer mixture, add the full 2 cups of powdered sugar.) Mix in the mini chocolate chips.

3. Turn out the mixture onto a large sheet of waxed paper. Use your hands to form it into a football shape.

4. Place the waxed paper on your serving plate. (It helps if the plate has sides—less mess!) Cover in sprinkles or chocolate chips, pressing them into the surface a little so they stick. Pull up the sides of the waxed paper to help you press the sprinkles or chips onto the sides of the dip. Pipe on the laces using melted white chocolate or some leftover frosting and chill until ready to serve. Cut off the excess waxed paper before serving. Store covered with plastic wrap in the refrigerator for up to 5 days.

5. Serve with pretzels, animal crackers, or cookies (or a spoon!).

Tip This dip is perfect for any occasion! You can make it into whatever shape you desire (like a heart with pink sprinkles for Valentine's Day) or make it into a simple cheese-ball shape instead.

White Chocolate Coconut Pie Fudge

Yield 36 pieces **Prep Time** 20 minutes **Bake Time** 22 minutes

My daughter was about four years old the first time I introduced her to a coconut dessert. It was Easter, and I'd made cupcakes with shredded coconut colored green for grass. She wouldn't go near them, claiming she hated coconut. A few years later she changed her tune and now we fight over any coconut desserts! This fudge is no exception. It's a white chocolate fudge that's easy to make, full of coconut, and it even has a crust.

1. Spray an 8 x 8-inch pan with cooking spray or line with foil and spray with cooking spray for easy cleanup.

2. Roll out the pie crust on a lightly floured surface to ¼ inch thick. Cut it into an 8¼-inch square. Place it in the prepared pan and press to fit. It will go up the sides slightly, but it will shrink a little during baking. Refrigerate for 30 minutes.

3. Preheat the oven to 350°F. When the crust is cold, pierce the bottom with the tines of a fork and bake for 19 to 22 minutes, until the edges are slightly brown. Cool while preparing the filling.

4. Place the sweetened condensed milk in a medium saucepan. Add ½ cup of the coconut and cook for 2 minutes over medium heat, stirring constantly. Add the white chocolate chips and stir constantly until melted together. Turn off the heat and add the coconut extract and salt. Immediately pour over the crust and top with the remaining coconut. Press the coconut lightly with your hands to adhere it to the surface of the fudge. Cool 1 hour at room temperature and then refrigerate for at least 4 hours until firm enough to cut. Store in an airtight container at room temperature for up to 5 days.

1 recipe All-Butter Pie Crust (page 64)

1 (14-ounce) can fat-free sweetened condensed milk

1 cup shredded sweetened coconut, divided

3 cups white chocolate chips

1 teaspoon imitation coconut extract

Pinch of salt

Tip This fudge is good even without the crust. Just pour the fudge mixture directly into the pan and refrigerate until set.

Apple Pie Cookies

Yield 30 cookies   **Prep Time** 20 minutes   **Chill Time** 30 minutes   **Bake Time** 11 minutes

The Fourth of July is one of my favorite holidays, and these Apple Pie Cookies are the perfect patriotic dessert for a potluck or BBQ!

½ cup (1 stick) unsalted butter, softened

½ cup packed brown sugar

¼ cup plus 2 tablespoons granulated sugar, divided

1 large egg

1 tablespoon vanilla extract

½ teaspoon baking soda

½ teaspoon salt

1½ teaspoons ground cinnamon, divided

1½ cups plus 1 tablespoon all-purpose flour, divided

1 large Granny Smith apple, peeled, cored, and diced small (just about 1½ cups)

½ cup water

Powdered sugar, for dusting

Tip If apple isn't your thing, you can simply place the cookie dough in the muffin pans, bake them, and then add a Hershey's Kiss or a mini peanut butter cup to the top when they come out of the oven. It's a great flavor twist!

1. Preheat the oven to 350°F. Spray three 12-cup mini muffin pans with cooking spray.

2. Cream together the butter, brown sugar, and ¼ cup of the granulated sugar in the bowl of a stand mixer fitted with the paddle attachment. Beat in the egg and vanilla.

3. In a medium bowl, whisk together the baking soda, salt, 1 teaspoon of the cinnamon, and 1½ cups of the flour. Add the dry ingredients to the wet and mix until combined. Cover with plastic wrap and refrigerate the dough for 30 minutes.

4. Place the diced apple in a small saucepan with the water. Cook over medium heat, stirring occasionally, just until the apples begin to turn translucent, about 5 minutes. Drain well and let cool for 10 minutes.

5. Scoop 1-tablespoon balls of cold cookie dough and place one in each cavity of the mini muffin pans. Press down to flatten slightly, and use your finger to create an indent in the centers for the apples.

6. Sprinkle the remaining 2 tablespoons granulated sugar, 1 tablespoon flour, and ½ teaspoon cinnamon over apples. Stir to combine. Place 1 teaspoon of apples in the hole of each cookie.

7. Bake for 9 to 11 minutes, until the cookies are browned. Cool at least 10 minutes before removing from the pan. It's easiest to remove them with a knife. Cool completely on a rack, then dust with powdered sugar before serving. Store in an airtight container at room temperature for up to 3 days.

Payday Candy Corn Rice Krispies Treats

Yield 24 squares   **Prep Time** 5 minutes   **Cook Time** 10 minutes   **Cool Time** 1 to 2 hours

Sometimes you come across some food combinations that totally blow your mind. Candy corn, a seemingly boring and too-sweet Halloween treat, becomes a magical food when mixed with certain things. When you eat candy corn together with peanuts, the flavor becomes just like a Payday candy bar! By adding those flavors, along with some peanut butter, to Rice Krispies treats, you get a dessert that actually has the taste and texture of a Payday . . . it's kind of amazing!

5 cups crispy rice cereal

1 cup peanuts

1 cup candy corn

¼ cup (1 stick) unsalted butter

6 cups mini marshmallows

½ cup creamy peanut butter

1. Line a 9 x 13-inch pan with foil and spray with cooking spray.

2. Place the cereal, peanuts, and candy corn in a large bowl. Set aside.

3. In another large microwave-safe bowl, place the butter, marshmallows, and peanut butter.

4. Microwave on high power in 30-second increments, stirring after each, until the everything is melted together. Remove from the microwave and pour the cereal mixture into the marshmallow mixture. Stir gently. Pour into the prepared pan. Press to fit. Be careful, the mixture will hot and sticky. It helps to spray your hands with cooking spray, so the treats won't stick to you.

5. Let sit at room temperature until cool. Cut into squares and serve. Store in an airtight container at room temperature for up to 3 days.

Tip Try to use fresh candy corn. The older it is, the harder it is to cut.

Pecan Pie Cinnamon Rolls

Yield 9 cinnamon rolls   **Prep Time** 45 minutes   **Rising Time** About 2 hours   **Bake Time** 28 minutes

If I could eat a cinnamon roll for breakfast every single day, I'd be a happy girl. I just love the flavors of cinnamon and butter and the yeasted dough, along with a really good frosting. In my quest to create new versions of cinnamon rolls, I came up with these pecan pie variations. The filling is made with the flavors of pecan pie: dark corn syrup and pecans. The frosting is also reminiscent of the pie and is made delicious with brown butter. Once you taste these cinnamon rolls, normal ones will never be the same again.

Dough

¾ cup nonfat milk

1 package active dry yeast (about 2¼ teaspoons)

⅓ cup granulated sugar

3 tablespoons unsalted butter, softened

½ teaspoon salt

1 large egg

3¼ cups all-purpose flour, plus more for dusting

Filling

5 tablespoons unsalted butter, softened

2 tablespoons dark corn syrup

⅔ cup packed brown sugar

1 tablespoon ground cinnamon

¼ teaspoon salt

2 tablespoons all-purpose flour

½ cup chopped pecans

Make the Dough

1. Place the milk in a microwave-safe measuring cup. Microwave on high for 45 to 60 seconds, until it's about 120°F. (The time will need to be adjusted depending on your microwave. You can use a candy or a meat thermometer to test the temperature.) Add the yeast and stir. Let it sit for a few minutes so the yeast can bloom.

2. Place the sugar, butter, salt, and egg in the bowl of a stand mixer fitted with the paddle attachment. Mix until the butter is distributed throughout the liquids, although it may be chunky. Pour in the milk-yeast mixture and stir for a few seconds.

3. Add 3 cups of flour and stir with the paddle attachment just until the mixture starts to stick to the paddle. Then replace the paddle with the dough hook. Continue mixing on low speed until the dough forms a ball in the center of the bowl. If the dough is still very sticky, you can add an additional ¼ cup of flour.

4. Spray a large bowl with cooking spray and place the dough ball in it. Lightly spray the top of the dough ball with cooking spray and cover the bowl with plastic wrap. Let sit for 2 to 4 hours until it doubles in size. Note: If your house is warm, the dough should rise with no problem. If it's cold in your house, it may take longer.

(continued on page 138)

Frosting

3 tablespoons unsalted butter

2 tablespoons dark corn syrup

1 cup powdered sugar

2 tablespoons nonfat milk

1 teaspoon vanilla extract

⅛ teaspoon maple extract

¼ cup chopped pecans

Tip Cut them smaller to make 12 cinnamon rolls and bake them in a 9 x 13-inch pan to feed a bigger crowd.

Make the Filling

1. In a large bowl, stir together the butter, corn syrup, brown sugar, cinnamon, salt, and flour until it forms a paste. Spray a 9-inch square or round pan or 9½-inch pie plate with cooking spray.

2. Once the dough is risen, roll it out on a lightly floured surface into a large rectangle, about 12 x 9 inches. Spread the filling as evenly as possible over the rectangle, making sure to reach to the sides so the outer rolls have enough filling. Sprinkle the pecans evenly over the filling.

3. Roll up the dough tightly from the long end. Slice it into 9 equal rounds. Place the rolls in the prepared pan.

4. At this point, you can let them rise for about 30 minutes to 1 hour at room temperature until they are swelling up in the pan and bake as directed. Or you can do what I do: cover with plastic wrap and refrigerate overnight until ready to bake.

5. When ready to bake, preheat the oven to 350°F. If the rolls have been in the refrigerator, remove them and let them warm up to room temperature while the oven is preheating. Remove the plastic wrap and bake for 23 to 28 minutes, until golden brown.

Make the Frosting

1. Melt the butter in a small saucepan over medium heat. Cook, stirring, until the butter turns brown. This happens after only a few minutes. Be sure to watch it so it doesn't burn. Transfer to a heat-safe medium bowl and cool for 15 minutes.

2. Once slightly cooled, stir the dark corn syrup into the butter. Whisk in the powdered sugar, milk, vanilla, and maple extract. Stir in the pecans. Pour over the warm cinnamon rolls.

Gingerbread Cheesecake Bars

Yield 24 bars   **Prep Time** 30 minutes   **Bake Time** 32 minutes   **Chill Time** 8 to 10 hours

I love gingerbread so much that I wish it were a year-round flavor. The spicy gingerbread in these bars pairs well with the cool cheesecake, and the crumble topping adds a finish of spice to in every bite.

Make the Gingerbread

1. Preheat the oven to 350°F. Spray a 9 x 13-inch pan with cooking spray or line with foil and spray with cooking spray for easy cleanup.

2. Whisk together the cinnamon, ginger, cloves, nutmeg, salt, baking soda, and flour in a medium bowl. Set aside.

3. Cream together the butter and brown sugar in the bowl of a stand mixer fitted with the paddle attachment. Mix in the molasses, egg, and vanilla. Mix in the dry ingredients and beat until the dough comes together. Press two-thirds of the dough into the prepared pan. It helps if you spray your hands with cooking spray first; the dough will be sticky.

(continued on page 141)

Gingerbread

½ teaspoon ground cinnamon

½ teaspoon ground ginger

¼ teaspoon ground cloves

¼ teaspoon ground nutmeg

⅛ teaspoon salt

¼ teaspoon baking soda

1¼ cups all-purpose flour

¼ cup (½ stick) unsalted butter, softened

⅓ cup packed brown sugar

3 tablespoons molasses

1 large egg

½ teaspoon vanilla extract

Cheesecake

8 ounces (1 package) cream cheese, at room temperature

¼ cup granulated sugar

⅓ cup sour cream, at room temperature

1 large egg, at room temperature

1 teaspoon vanilla extract

Make the Cheesecake

1. Wash mixing bowl and paddle attachment then reattach them to the mixer. Beat the cream cheese until smooth. Beat in the sugar and sour cream. Add the egg and mix well. Stir in the vanilla. Pour over the crust.

Make the Crumble

1. Mix together all the crumble ingredients with a hand mixer. The mixture will be very crumbly. Sprinkle over the cheesecake and press slightly to set.

2. Bake for 28 to 32 minutes, until the cheesecake is set. Let cool to room temperature, then cover with plastic wrap and refrigerate overnight before cutting. Store in an airtight container in the refrigerator for up to 4 days.

Tip Add some red and green sprinkles in with the crumble topping for a festive holiday treat!

Crumble

2 tablespoons unsalted butter, softened

¼ cup packed brown sugar

½ cup all-purpose flour

½ teaspoon ground cinnamon

¼ teaspoon ground ginger

¼ teaspoon ground cloves

¼ teaspoon ground nutmeg

Caramel Spice Cake Blondies

Yield 24 bars   Prep Time 15 minutes   Cook Time 25 minutes

The base of this blondie is one of my favorite recipes of all time. It's always good no matter what! And, because of all that brown sugar, they stay soft for days. The spices in these blondies make them perfect for fall and winter—they have the warmth of the holidays in every bite!

1 teaspoon baking powder

¼ teaspoon salt

2 teaspoons ground cinnamon

¼ teaspoon ground cloves

¼ teaspoon ground allspice

¼ teaspoon ground nutmeg

½ teaspoon ground ginger

2 cups all-purpose flour

2 cups packed brown sugar

½ cup (1 stick) unsalted butter

2 large eggs

1 tablespoon vanilla extract

1¾ cups unwrapped chocolate-covered caramel candies (such as Rolos or Caramel Hershey's Kisses; about 50), divided

1. Preheat the oven to 350°F. Spray a 9 x 13-inch pan with cooking spray or line with foil and spray with cooking spray for easy cleanup.

2. Whisk together the dry ingredients: baking powder, salt, cinnamon, cloves, allspice, nutmeg, ginger, and flour. Set aside.

3. Cream together the brown sugar and butter in the bowl of a stand mixer fitted with a paddle attachment. Add the eggs and vanilla and beat until combined. Add the dry ingredients and mix until smooth.

4. Stir in 1 cup of the chocolate-caramel candies, about 30.

5. Press the dough into the prepared pan. The dough will be sticky, so spray your hands with cooking spray to keep it from sticking to you. Sprinkle the remaining ¾ cup of chocolate-caramel candies (about 20) over the top and press lightly to make them stick to the surface.

6. Bake at for 22 to 25 minutes. Be careful not to overcook—the center will still be jiggly when you take these out of the oven and they will finish cooking and firming up as they cool. They taste best a little underdone. Cool completely before slicing into squares.

Tip These would also be yummy with white chocolate chips instead of the caramel candies!

Pumpkin Pie Magic Bars

Yield 24 bars   **Prep Time** 15 minutes   **Bake Time** 35 minutes   **Cool Time** 2 to 4 hours

Giving a normal everyday dessert (like a magic bar) a makeover for a holiday is one of the things I love most about my job. Magic bars are so easy to change up, so adding the flavors of any holiday is easy. These pumpkin pie magic bars are made with yummy fall ingredients: toffee, pumpkin, and pecans all layered on top of a gingersnap crust. If you've never tried pumpkin with gingersnaps before, this is a great place to start. You're in for a treat!

1. Preheat the oven to 350°F. Spray a 9 x 9-inch pan with cooking spray or line with foil and spray with cooking spray for easy cleanup.

2. Grind the gingersnaps to a fine crumb in a food processor; you should have about 1½ cups of crumbs. Place cookie crumbs in a medium bowl and mix with the sugar and melted butter. Press into the prepared pan.

3. Sprinkle the white chocolate chips, pecans, coconut, and toffee over the top of the crust.

4. Whisk together the pumpkin puree, sweetened condensed milk, and pumpkin pie spice in a small bowl or measuring cup and pour over the top of the bars. The mixture will just barely cover; use a spatula to carefully spread it to the edges.

5. Bake for 29 to 35 minutes, until the edges have started to brown. Cool completely before cutting. Store in an airtight container in the refrigerator for up to 4 days.

Tip Different brands of sweetened condensed milk come in different thicknesses. If it's too thick to be pourable, you can transfer it to a microwave-safe bowl and heat it on high for 10 to 20 seconds until it becomes a little thinner.

25 gingersnap cookies, or as needed

2 tablespoons granulated sugar

5 tablespoons unsalted butter, melted

1 cup white chocolate chips

1 cup chopped pecans

¼ cup shredded sweetened coconut

¼ cup toffee bits

¼ cup pumpkin puree

½ cup fat-free sweetened condensed milk

½ teaspoon pumpkin pie spice

Brownie Peppermint Bark

Yield 4 cups   **Prep Time** 15 minutes   **Bake Time** 11 minutes   **Chill Time** about 2 hours

Bark is my favorite thing to make at the holidays. It's so easy! We love peppermint bark in our house (my daughter even came up with an Oreo Peppermint Bark last year that became one of the most popular recipes on my blog), and the brownie crust on this treat takes it over the top. The brownie crust is thinner than a regular brownie, so with the peppermint bark layer on top it's the perfect Christmas candy!

½ cup vegetable oil

1 cup granulated sugar

½ cup unsweetened cocoa powder

1 large egg

¼ teaspoon salt

1 teaspoon vanilla extract

1 cup all-purpose flour

11½ to 12 ounces white chocolate chips (about 2 cups)

½ cup crushed candy canes (about 6 regular-sized)

1. Preheat the oven to 350°F. Spray a 9 x 13-inch pan with cooking spray or line with foil and spray with cooking spray for easy cleanup.

2. In a large bowl, stir together the vegetable oil, sugar, and cocoa powder with a wooden spoon. Stir in the egg, salt, and vanilla. Carefully stir in the flour. The mixture will be thick.

3. Spread the batter in a thin layer in the prepared pan. It's easiest to use your hands, but since the dough will be sticky, you should spray them with cooking spray. Bake for 9 to 11 minutes, until the brownies are cooked through; a toothpick inserted along the edge of the pan should come out clean. Cool completely in the pan before continuing.

4. Melt the white chocolate chips in a microwave-safe bowl. Heat them on 50 percent power in 30-second increments, stirring after each, until smooth. Spread in an even layer over the brownie crust. Sprinkle the crushed candy canes over the top. Refrigerate to harden, then break into pieces. Store in an airtight container in the refrigerator for up to 1 week. Best eaten at room temperature.

Tip This recipe is not limited to candy canes! Use any candy you love. Or dress it up for different holidays by using colored sprinkles. The sky is the limit for this recipe.

Index

Acknowledgments

If you had told me years ago that I'd have a successful blog and be writing a cookbook, I would have laughed. But I've learned I can do so much more than I ever thought I could. Doors have opened that I didn't know existed, and now here I am, writing my first cookbook. It's a little bit surreal and a lot amazing.

Writing a cookbook is like having a baby. It's a long process, a challenging experience, and it can't be done alone. I've had so much support over the past several months!

I have to begin by thanking everyone who has ever clicked onto Crazy for Crust. Without you, my faithful readers, I wouldn't even have known that a cookbook was something I wanted to do. Thank you for reading, for commenting, for sharing, and for enjoying this slice of life with me.

I want to thank my blogging friends and community. You know who you are; you've touched my life in ways I cannot even express. Without you, this job would not be as fun, satisfying, or fulfilling as it is. Thank you for your unwavering friendship and support!

To everyone who helped me with this book—testing recipes and tasting them—I am so appreciative! Thank you for letting me unload my pies and cookies and cakes so that I didn't eat any more of them (because I did eat my fare share . . . and then some).

I want to thank my editor, Katherine Furman, and the team at Ulysses Press for having the faith in me to write this book . . . and for putting up with my hundreds of questions with so much patience!

Thank you to my parents, who have always been my #1 fans. From visiting the blog each day to liking every single Facebook post and even joining Instagram without a smartphone, you both have supported me more than I can ever thank you for.

A special thank you to all of my in-laws. Thank you for supporting me from day one on this journey. I'm so happy that I can call you my family.

Jordan, I want to say a special thank you to you. It's not easy to have a mom who's working a full-time job and writing a cookbook, and you handled it amazingly. You are the best daughter a mom could have, and I'm so lucky I got you. Seeing your sweet smile every day kept me going.

And last but most certainly not least, thank you to my husband, Mel. You are an amazing dad, an even better husband, and the best friend a girl could have. Thank you for always believing in me even when I didn't believe in myself. Thank you for doing the dishes, putting up with all the chaos, and being the shoulder I needed so much during this process. Back in that CS030A classroom so many years ago I subconsciously knew you were special, and I was right. This book, this life, is only possible because I have you to share it with.

And finally, thank you to all of you for buying this book. I hope that you enjoy it, that you create memories with the food created in it, and that, in the words of Ernestine Ulmer, you realize that life is uncertain, so you eat dessert first.

About the Author

Dorothy Kern is the founder, writer, photographer, and baker behind the popular dessert blog *Crazy for Crust*. She started blogging in 2010 to showcase her love of pie, but quickly realized she loved baking all sorts of desserts. Her blog evolved into what it is today: a baking site full of delicious desserts that are sometimes crazy, often have a crust, and are always served with a slice of life. Dorothy's creations have been featured by *The Huffington Post*, *Everyday with Rachael Ray* magazine, and *Woman's World* magazine. She lives in Northern California with her husband and daughter, and is rarely seen without her Kindle or her iPhone. Find her online at www.crazyforcrust.com, and show your love by posting pictures of your creations from this book to social media using #dessertmashups.

Kirkpatrick Photography